RUNNING ON
EMPTY

A HANDBOOK FOR UNDERSTANDING AND SURVIVING THE ENERGY CRISIS

PHILLIP J. GREENE

ISBN: 1-4392-3302-0
ISBN-13: 9781439233023
LCCN: 2009902498

Visit www. booksurge.com to order more copies.

Crisis (Kri'sis) A crucial point or situation in the course of anything; a turning point. An unstable condition in political, international or economic affairs in which an abrupt or decisive change is impending.

— From *the American Heritage Dictionary of the English Language*

DEDICATION

To our children, our grandchildren, and their children yet to come. In the midst of gloom and doom about this period of time, about world economics, and about the overheating of this glorious planet, a golden opportunity has arrived. Your generations have the chance to become good stewards of planet earth, but it will require all your knowledgeable interest and creativity. It is my fondest hope that you will rise to this challenge, and with your fellow human beings, you will live well and nurture the earth so that it can nurture human kind for thousands of years.

May 2009

CONTENTS

ACKNOWLEDGEMENTS

My research took me to Kenneth S. Deffeyes' book, *Hubbert's Peak*: *The Impending World Oil Shortage*, as well as his updated version, *Beyond Oil: The View from Hubbert's Peak.* I also consulted Richard Heinberg's book, *The Party's Over: Oil, War and the Fate of Industrial Societies,* for his view of what can happen if we take no heed of the warnings of what a world without oil would look like.

I am indebted to my wife, Margaret (Peggy) Greene, for her encouragement, tireless help, and long hours spent sifting through enormous amounts of information regarding ways to conserve energy and save money. She was instrumental in developing the extensive list describing the many energy-savings ideas of which we can all avail ourselves to make contributions to weaning ourselves from fossil fuels.

I would like to thank Saint Louis architect John Kemper for sharing his experience with ground source geothermal heat pumps, and Rosemary Latshaw for sharing her experience with the installation of a solar photovoltaic system. In addition I am grateful to Gery Hawkins for searching for technical errors.

I am indebted to my editor, Peter Gelfan, for his help and excellent suggestions for organizing my thoughts and ideas.

I am indebted to the United States Congress, who, after many years and several administrations, finally decided to do something constructive for our great country, by adding measures to the recently passed financial bail-out legislation that promises to kick-start the renewable energy industry. It's about time.

Lastly, I am indebted to President Barak Obama, whose administration is dedicated to implementing programs that promise to change the direction of the country's energy policy, or more aptly, its lack of an energy policy, by encouraging the development of renewable energy sources to replace fossil fuels as our main energy source.

INTRODUCTION

Can you imagine a world without oil? If you know all of the ways that oil impacts our modern world, you will understandably have a difficult time imagining such a world. Our automobiles that give us our freedom of mobility, the food we eat, the products we buy and sell, our warm comfortable homes, all are made possible by the ease with which we can obtain oil and other fossil fuels. If you have traveled to undeveloped third world countries, you can begin to understand what a world without oil would be like. And yet even the poorest of these countries have cars, things made of plastic, and many things that are dependent upon oil. The closest one can come to a place completely devoid of anything related to oil is the Amazon jungle where remote tribes with little or no contact with the outside world reside. This is not a world in which any of us would want to live.

Is it Empty?

In this country, the closest one can come to a world without oil is the way in which the Amish live. Their circumstances are not dire, and they flourish because they have settled in a land with plenty of water and rich soil that grows plenty of food. They make their own clothing, usually from natural fibers like cotton, containing no petroleum-based synthetic fibers, but probably made in factories somewhere, powered by electricity generated by coal. They still use horse-drawn buggies for transportation, although some do own cars these days. They plow their fields with horses and often have no electricity in their homes. Some compromise with electric lights in their barns, but in their homes, they often use kerosene lanterns for light and coal or propane for heating and cooking. Even the Amish use some fossil fuels. Their lifestyle is a matter of choice, unlike those living in impoverished third world countries in sub-Saharan Africa. Would you choose to live that way?

Fortunately, we have an abundance of electricity to light our homes, gas or oil to heat them, and electricity to cool them. We currently have plenty of gasoline to run our cars, allowing us to go wherever we like. We have an abundant supply of electricity or natural gas to cook our food, and all we need to do to get our food is drive a short distance to the supermarket. Markets are always full of delicious and nutritious foods, even out of season fruits and vegetables. If we want to travel, we can hop on an airplane and be almost anywhere on the continent in a matter of a few hours. Our appliances, televisions, iPods, computers, clothing, and home improvement products are easily purchased from huge nearby stores offering thousands of products at reasonable prices. Our jobs are easy to get to simply by jumping in the family car. If you work a long distance from your home, it's not a problem, just a slight inconvenience and a little more commuting time. Contrast this life style with that of sub-Saharan Africa or even the Amish. Without cheap fossil fuels, or a reasonably priced substitute, our current lifestyle would not exist.

Do we have an energy crisis? The above definition from the dictionary hits the nail on the head. We are most certainly at a turning point. If something happens to others and not to you, it's a doggone shame, and we call it a news item. Something that directly affects you personally and not someone else is a crisis. We do have an energy crisis. It isn't like watching the World Trade Center come down on 911, but it is occurring to us now. Because it is happening in slow motion and not on TV, it doesn't seem to be real.

Past Energy Crises—Then and Now

We have had several energy crises before. Some readers may not be old enough to remember, but back in 1973, we had one that should have been very instructive to us. Interestingly, we also had a stock market crash then too. What caused the energy crisis then was the major oil producing countries, all members of the Organization of Petroleum Exporting Countries (OPEC), placing an embargo on all shipments of oil to the United States. They did this because we supported Israel in their Yom Kippur War in which Syria and Egypt attacked Israel. It was the first time a country, or group of countries like OPEC, used oil as a weapon in the world of diplomacy and war. It is unlikely to be the last. Sadly, we didn't learn much from it. We should have set different policies with regard to energy and started down the path toward energy independence. Instead we put all of our eggs in the fossil fuel basket. Our mantra became drill, baby drill.

A funny thing happened on the way to our most recent energy crisis in 2008. Over a period of eight presidential administrations, headed by both political parties, very little besides talk was done to acknowledge our dependence on a vital strategic commodity controlled by OPEC, an organization of seven Arab countries, plus Iran, Ecuador, Indonesia, Angola, Venezuela, and Nigeria. Which of those states do you think are our friends?

In the 2008 presidential election campaign, politicians argued that we should drill more wells, but the oil companies did nothing in spite of making huge profits. They said we did not have enough refinery capacity to process more oil, but they didn't build more refineries. The president did go to Saudi Arabia to beg his Arab friends there to *please, please* increase production and send us some more oil, but they did little to help us. We the people of the United States of gas-guzzlers—what did we do? Nothing, except pay the bill for higher and higher gasoline prices and try to unload our SUVs. The trouble is no one wanted those dinosaurs. People were ready to throw a mattress in the back and turn them into guest rooms for the in-laws. Vacant lots sprouted SUVs with "For Sale" signs on them.

The truth is that we did finally do something in 2008, after the price of oil and gas went up to levels never before experienced in history. What we did was to drive less, buy less gasoline, and find new ways to get to work. Suddenly the price went down again. I guess we showed those oil companies a thing or two. They can't bully us. There is no energy crisis—at least not now, is there?

What Crisis?

Unfortunately, in spite of the ups and downs of the price of oil and gas, nothing has changed. What really caused lower gas and oil prices was a complicated series of events. People did drive less, but a worldwide financial crisis also left people without jobs and less money to spend on expensive gas. The economy was the culprit. In spite of lower prices, we still have an energy crisis, and it is not going away. In fact, by the time you read this, gas prices may have returned to those stratospheric 2008 levels. Part of the reason for the wide swings in the price of oil and gasoline in 2008 was the result of speculators gambling that the price of oil was going up. There was no shortage. Amazingly, some brokerage houses actually bought crude oil and put it in storage tanks waiting for the price to skyrocket. The federal government also released some of our strategic oil reserves held against a natural catastrophe or war, causing a slight decrease in price. When prices didn't go back up—in fact, they went lower—some of those speculators went belly up. Good riddance.

It's the Teeth!

When people mistakenly think the energy crisis is just about the price of gasoline, it brings to mind a story about a postman who had a bull dog on his route that took great exception to his intrusion into its domain. He was reluctant to deliver mail to the front porch where the dog growled and bared its teeth. The mailman got into the habit of leaving the mail on a large fence post at the front gate. One day the homeowner met the mailman with the news that he had gotten the dog neutered, and it was OK to come into the yard to deliver the mail. The mailman replied to the owner, "You don't understand. It's the teeth."

We need to understand what is going to bite us. The teeth that will be biting us in the posterior are represented by the finite nature of fossil fuels and disappearance of them in the not too distant future. It's not the price, although the price will undoubtedly increase, nipping us twice. The energy crisis is not about the *price* of oil or gasoline. Let me repeat that. *The price of oil is not what the energy crisis is about. It is about the fact that we are rapidly using up the world's supply of fossil fuels, which includes oil.* The cost of fuel is certainly important to us, but not as important as completely running out of this important commodity.

Are we really running out of oil? How do we know? If so, when will it happen? How about those other fossil fuels, like coal and natural gas? Are they running out too? Why hasn't the government told us and done something about it? Because it hasn't really bitten us in the rump yet, that's why. It nipped us a teeny bit in the summer of 2008, but it didn't break the skin. The next time it rears its ugly head, we probably will lose some body parts.

Want to Chance Running Out?

The book will address these questions and more. The various alternative fuels with the most promise will be discussed. Their importance as replacements in the transition toward a world free of fossil fuels will be examined. A list of actions that people can take in their everyday lives will be presented. They are actions that will save energy and money for the family as well as reduce our country's dependency on fossil fuels. Many require little or no investment and can produce results almost immediately. All are aimed at helping us weather the transition to alternative energies. Read on to find out how energy became a crisis for us and what we can do about it.

CHAPTER 1: IS THERE *REALLY* AN ENERGY CRISIS?

Not Fossil Fuel?

Just what are fossil fuels? The big three are oil, natural gas, and coal. There are other products derived from them, but they are the primary fossil fuels on which our economy runs and depends. The term *fossil fuel* refers to fuels originating from the remains of ancient plants and animals buried deep in the earth's crust hundreds of millions of years ago, transformed into hydrocarbons by the earth's heat and great pressure. They are not the result of dinosaurs dying and decaying as some suggest, but in the case of oil, they result from microscopic zooplankton deposited on ancient ocean floors. Coal is the result of plant matter from ancient forests being buried and subjected to great heat and pressure. Natural gas results from the same basic process, except that gas is the result of higher temperature and pressure. Gas is often found together with coal and oil. They all contain a mix of hydrogen and carbon in differing amounts and are therefore called hydrocarbons. Combustion of fossil fuels generates pollution, most of which is carbon dioxide

(CO_2). The hydrogen and carbon, when combined with oxygen, are what burns. Fossil fuels are finite commodities, and our use of them affects everything throughout our country and the world. Modern society can't exist without them. Unfortunately, one of these days they will be gone.

How Can We Tell That We Are Running Out?

The evidence that we are running out of oil is difficult to pin down, hence the confusion and controversy about the subject. Since oil occurs entirely underground, the surest way to tell what is left is to drill a well and pump it out. There are highly sophisticated techniques for searching for deposits and determining how much there is below the surface, but ultimately drilling is the only foolproof way to tell what is left.

Few New Discoveries of Large Deposits

There have been few new large oil fields discovered in the United States in the past ten years. The most recent large field discovered was called the Bakken field, which is located in North Dakota, Montana, and Saskatchewan, Canada. Bakken covers a large area, but it is a very shallow deposit, less than ten feet deep. Drilling the field requires some unusual techniques that are very expensive. It requires drilling down to the oil-bearing strata and then getting the drill head to turn and drill horizontally.

Oil companies hold leases in the Gulf of Mexico that have not been pursued. With the price of oil hitting unprecedented levels in 2008, one would expect these leases to be drilled if they were expected to produce a reasonable supply of oil at a reasonable price. Mexico is one of our major suppliers of oil. The production of Mexico's Cantarell field in the Gulf, their largest, has been declining, signaling that it may be running dry. Older fields in other countries are showing their age too. In view of these two seemingly unusual and unconnected situations, the lack of exploration and Mexico's largest field becoming depleted, one could be led to believe that there may not be a lot of new oil to be found.

Increasing Use of Tertiary Recovery

The increasing use of tertiary recovery methods for "depleted wells" is another sign that it may not be worth drilling new wells in an existing field in spite of higher oil prices. Tertiary recovery refers to the third stage in the productive life of an oil well. In the first stage, the oil almost squirts out of the ground on its own or is at least easy to pump. In the second stage, artificial mud is pumped into the well forcing the oil out. In the third, or tertiary stage, carbon dioxide (CO_2) gas is pumped into the well to force the last drops of oil out of the ground. Pumping CO_2 into an older well to recover more oil is less expensive than drilling an entirely new well, but this process often involves drilling two holes on either side of an existing well in which to pump the CO_2. The amounts that can be recovered in this manner are a gamble, much like drilling a new well.

Increased Interest in Unconventional Sources

When the price of oil reached $147 a barrel in 2008, interest in oil sands and shales, called unconventional oil, increased considerably, and the mining of it became active. It is a difficult type of oil extraction and very polluting to the atmosphere and ground water. If regular wells could be drilled in locations easier to access, oil in sand or shale would not be of interest because of the cost of extracting it. After the 2008 price surge abated and prices went down again, most of these operations ceased or were put on hold.

Peak Oil Theory

In 1956 geologist M. King Hubbert predicted that the production of oil in the world would peak in the not too distant future, after which a rapid decline would occur until the oil was gone. He coined the term "peak oil," and predicted that the peak would be reached in 1970. He was very nearly right. A few new discoveries have moved the date forward, but in the 1980s, production began to level off and then start downward in a classic bell-shaped curve. The slowing of production can mean that the price is too low to cover production costs plus a profit, or the field is becoming depleted. Demand enters into the equation too. This complicates determining the exact time at which production will decline for good because of the depletion of wells. Assessing reserves is problematical for several reasons. The actual time at which production peaks is elusive. The point is that it will happen sooner or later.

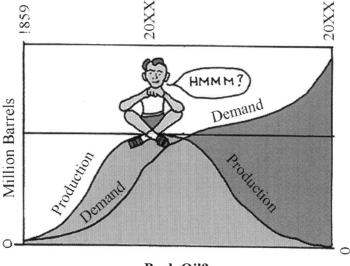

Peak Oil?

The concept of Peak Oil is recognized as real by the U.S. National Academy of Science, the U.S. National Academy of Engineering, the U.S. General Accountability Office (GAO), the U.S. Congressional Budget Office, the U.S. Army Corps of Engineers, the National Petroleum Council, and even some major oil companies. The problem is getting a consensus with regard to when we reach that magic point in time. No one seems to know for sure. Estimates change almost daily. Many oil-producing nations find it beneficial for political reasons to be secretive about their reserves.

Differing Views

A new report in 2008 from the United Kingdom Industry Task Force on Peak Oil and Energy, an alliance of eight British companies, including an oil company, reported that oil production will peak between 2011 and 2013. According to that report, there is evidence that oil-producing countries are beginning to regard oil and gas as resources to be kept in reserve for their own future use, suggesting that they see it as a diminishing resource too.

OPEC sees the peak of oil production as happening between 2020 and 2030. Their assessment of reserves still in the ground is unreliable, because they are required by OPEC to limit their production to a certain percentage of their reserves. They tend to overestimate their reserves in order to be allowed to increase their allotment and produce more if they wish. Industry experts call their predictions "political data," and view their reports as being suspect. The UK Industry Task Force report may be closer to the truth.

The International Energy Alliance (IEA), founded during the 1973–74 energy crisis, is an intergovernmental organization that acts as an energy policy advisor to twenty-eight member countries. It was established to ensure reliable, affordable, and clean energy for the citizens of member countries. Their opinion is that the peak will be in 2030. Oddly enough, the IEA had done no studies to assess when the peak might occur until 2008. What were they using for their assessment of reserves from 1974 until 2008? Did they just accept the assessment of anyone that came up with one, like OPEC? There was a time from 1985 to 1988 when the reported oil reserves of OPEC jumped dramatically, almost doubling with no new oil field discoveries, and then leveling off. Did the assessment technology improve so dramatically as to cause this change, or were producers blowing smoke up our backside? The likelihood is that they were cooking the books to obtain better quotas, since quotas are set from reserve numbers. From more trustworthy numbers, it seems that oil production peaked around 1970 and began to decline as predicted by M. King Hubbert. Everyone has an opinion, and they are all over the map.

The estimated date of peak oil is a moving target. The fact remains that our consumption of oil, and that of the rest of the world, continues to grow steadily along with the world population. Many developing countries, especially China and India, are experiencing new growth of the middle class because of the world market. These newly affluent people want to own automobiles and live in nice houses just like us, and growing numbers of them already do. Their consumption of fuel grows right along with their numbers who move up in the economy.

Dubious Theories

Dubious theories abound. It's difficult to know who to believe. Politicians, a group that hardly anyone believes, just muddy the water. Too often their reelection relies on donations from companies or individuals with some kind of vested interest. We have to look at all of the evidence and make judgments based on what we find. We must look closely at who provides the information and what biases they might have, because many industry experts do have a dog in the fight.

A group of Russian geologists maintains that oil is not the product of fossilized zooplankton. They hold that oil is the product of an abiotic process occurring in the molten core of the earth. Abiotic means not made from living biological organisms. Their theory is that oil is created in the molten core of the earth and is forced up through the earth's crust. The truly amazing part of this theory is their assertion that oil is renewable, and it will continue to bubble up through the earth's crust indefinitely due to the centrifugal force of the earth's rotation. Few serious scientists agree with this theory.

Drilling the Arctic National Wildlife Reserve

During the 2008 political campaign, some politicians were preaching that all we need to do to break away from our dependence on foreign oil is to let the oil companies drill in the Arctic National Wildlife Refuge (ANWR) and off of our coastlines. ANWR is reputed to have 100 billion barrels that could be recovered if we allowed drilling there. We probably would not see any oil from ANWR for about ten years. That puts us at 2019. The oil reported in ANWR represents about a 1.5-year supply at current rates of consumption. Bear in mind that world consumption is not leveling off, but continues upward in a straight line. After that is gone, then what? We still will need some replacement for fossil oil. Is it worth destroying a pristine area for a year and a half's supply? For those who claim we should still drill there and that the oil can be recovered with little damage to the wildlife reserve, I ask how the Exxon Valdez spill turned out. It happened twenty years ago, and so far, Exxon has spent over two billion dollars on a clean up and lawsuits. The spill is still not totally cleaned up, and Exxon claims it is not their responsibility to do so.

The 2009 April issue of *National Geographic* magazine reports that since the Exxon Valdez oil spill in 1989, 439 additional major spills occurred throughout the world. The rate of spills has improved since the United Nations has agreed on a phase out of single-hulled tankers like the Exxon Valdez by the year 2010.

Offshore Drilling—How Much Is Out There?

Drilling offshore in the Gulf of Mexico and along our east and west shore lines has gotten a lot of press, particularly during the 2008 presidential campaign. Why haven't we allowed more drilling offshore? If there are drillable deposits offshore, they are costly and difficult to develop. It would take about ten years before a drop of oil came to market. The amount of oil that is out there remains a mystery. The true proof of the pudding is in the drilling, to use a badly confused metaphor. In ten years, the optimistic scenarios predict that oil production will be heading toward depletion. Will the ANWR and offshore sites sustain us at that time and for how long? Are we feeling lucky? It seems like a poor gamble. Why don't we just develop some nonfossil alternative fuels and use every alternative we can to make the transition to clean fuel. Wouldn't it be great to be done with OPEC, Russia, and Venezuela once and for all and tell them to take their oil and shove it?

Off Shore Drilling

Drilling is one thing. Discovery is another. First you have to find where drilling is probably going to yield some oil. That takes time and money. If it turns out to be a dry hole, the rig has to be moved to another site to try again. A deep well, offshore oil rig costs about a billion dollars a copy, and that's before they drop the drill bit to the ocean floor and start drilling. Those deep well rigs cost about $200,000 a day to operate.

Want to rent one? That will run $600,000 a day. Then there's the refinery problem. We do not have enough of them. It takes years to build one, and they would not bring any oil to the market any time soon. We do not have enough drilling rigs either. Ship yards would be hard pressed to build enough offshore drilling rigs to really make a big difference anytime soon in the price of oil at the pump. Even if they could produce the oil drilling rigs, it would be years before we got any oil from them. Yes, drilling does create jobs, and that's a good thing, but it will not get us a lot of oil in the near future. It also fails to recognize the elephant in the room: global warming and atmospheric pollution.

With regard to oil, the question is not where can we get cheap oil from sources close to home? The real questions we need to answer are how can we cure our addiction to and insatiable consumption of fossil fuels? How can we find substitutes for them that will support our energy-intensive lifestyle and still prevent global warming? The sooner we address these questions the better off we will be.

Supply and Demand—Who Calls the Tune?

The United States is not the only country addicted to oil. The new world economy, in which all countries of the world can participate, runs on fossil fuels. Cheap labor and cheap fuels make it possible for goods to be shipped from the farthest corners of the world to anywhere on the planet. (See Thomas Friedman, *The World is Flat*, Farrar, Straus and Giroux 2005, and *The World is Flat, Hot, and Crowded*, Farrar, Straus and Giroux, 2008). Competition for oil on the world market is growing because of developing countries like China, India, and Brazil. China with its 1.37 billion people is an enormous market, as is India with just over one billion people. Consumption of fossil fuels in just these two countries will only continue to increase. Oil on the open market will always go to the highest bidder. We cannot rely on a stable, secure supply at low prices. Producers can charge whatever the market will allow.

Supply and demand unfortunately are not always reliable indicators. The wide price fluctuations of 2008 were not due to market forces alone. Speculators interfered with the normal market function. Producers can muck about by manipulating production to affect price. OPEC's decision to lower production late in 2008 is a case in point. Because of a global financial crisis, however, the effect wasn't quite what they expected, and prices didn't rise as much as they wanted. We should be careful what we wish for. If prices are too low, producers may decide to sit on the sidelines and wait for the price to go up to their comfort level, thus resulting in shortages. Nothing is simple.

In summation, we do have an energy crisis, and we are at a turning point. An unstable situation exists in the Middle East, a major source of our energy. Depletion of major oil fields appears to be taking place. Most scientists agree that oil will disappear sometime in the future, although they don't all agree when that will occur. We must become energy independent to the extent that our needs and our technology allow. Every possible energy alternative must be pursued. There is no magic bullet out there in terms of replacing fossil fuels. We will likely have to continue some fossil fuels until the alternative industries can get up to speed.

CHAPTER 2: GLOBAL WARMING

Complicating the issues surrounding peak oil and the energy crisis debate is a crisis involving global warming and air pollution. Global warming gives us yet another reason to eliminate fossil fuels from our major sources of energy. Developing renewable nonfossil fuels has an added benefit of reducing greenhouse gases in the atmosphere. Global warming has nothing to do with the depletion of our fossil fuels, except that our continuing reliance on them makes global warming a greater problem, hence our discussion here.

The CO_2 Problem

The overwhelming majority of the scientific community believes that human activity contributes to global warming. It appears that some of the contrarian views stem from politics or relationships with fossil fuel producers rather than science. However, there is a substantial body of serious scientists that refute the role of human activity in global warming.

Many natural phenomena unrelated to human activity can affect our environment. First, the earth's elliptical orbit places the planet at varying distances from the sun throughout its travel through space, causing it to be warmer or cooler depending on the distance from earth to the sun. The earth's tilt and the warping of the plane of its orbit also cause variations in the earth's atmospheric temperature. When the earth is warmed or cooled by these natural causes, the effect can cause either the warming or cooling to accelerate because of the absorption or release of CO_2 by the ocean. Warm water releases CO_2 and cool water absorbs it.

The release of additional CO_2 by the ocean after a warming period is a crucial point in the argument that global warming is not caused by human activity. The naysayers cite data that indicates that warming occurs a long time before the CO_2 build up, not the other way around. Therefore, cause and effect are reversed. The confusion produced by natural causes of global warming stems from the assertion that CO_2 can cause warming of the atmosphere. The non-human theorists say that it doesn't and that it is warming that causes CO_2.

It is undeniable that human activity sends vast amounts of CO_2 into the atmosphere. If carbon dioxide from natural causes affects the atmosphere, causing warming, why doesn't the CO_2 that humans produce affect it too? Presented with this argument, the believers in the natural theory of warming counter by saying that CO_2 is good and more is even better. It is true that plants and trees need CO_2 to grow, and they absorb it while releasing oxygen in the process. Sadly, when the forests are cut down, this natural absorption of CO_2 is interrupted.

Support for the assertion that human activity causes global warming comes from the Intergovernmental Panel on Climate Change (IPCC) and the Environmental Defense Fund (EDF). The IPCC is made up of government members and scientists and was set up by the World Meteorological Organization under the United Nations Environment Program. The EDF is a broad-based international nonprofit environmental advocacy group of business people and scientists. Both the IPCC and the EDF believe that global warming is real and that it is indeed related to human behavior. They are joined in their belief by a large body of climatologists and scientists.

Because it is a governmental organization, the IPCC has been criticized as being biased. They have been accused of cherry picking data and ignoring that which doesn't support their position. For the contrarian view, see the Web site for the Nongovernmental International Panel on Climate Change (NIPCC). If that doesn't confuse you enough, go to the No Smog Blog at www.nosmogblog.com where the NIPCC is in turn denounced.

Don't be put off by all this alphabet soup. If you read much about climate change, you will run across these endless capital letter combinations again.

As recently as April 24, 2009, it has come to light, in an article in the New York Times that the Global Climate Coalition led an aggressive lobbying and public information campaign for more than a decade against the idea that emissions of heat trapping gases could lead to global warming. This group represented industries whose profits were tied to fossil fuels, and their funds for their public disinformation campaign came from the oil, coal and auto industries to the tune of $1.68 million in 1997. That was the year the Kyoto Protocol was negotiated. The United States did not sign that protocol. I wonder why.

Make My Day

A document filed in a federal lawsuit revealed that the coalition's own scientific and technical experts were advising that the science backing the role of greenhouse gases in global warming could not be refuted. This was reported as long ago as 1995 in an internal document.

Greenhouse gases do help make planet earth habitable by keeping our atmosphere warm enough to support life. Without it, we would return to the ice age and be unable to grow food. However, too much of a good thing can be a problem too, resulting in the earth becoming too warm. Polar ice caps are already melting, and sea levels rising faster than predicted.

The two most abundant greenhouse gases are CO_2 and methane, with the preponderance being CO_2. Methane, the second most abundant, is by far the most dangerous. Methane is a more efficient greenhouse gas, trapping more heat than CO_2, and accelerating warming faster. Scientists predict that if temperatures rise to a certain level, say +2 to +2.5 degrees Fahrenheit, a lethal amount of methane, trapped in frozen bogs in the Arctic. Could be released, causing a natural catastrophe. There are other greenhouse gases in lesser amounts, but no less toxic. These gases are caused by many sources, some of which are naturally occurring, like volcanoes. We can't do much about volcanoes, but we can slow or stop the production of greenhouse gases caused by our activities.

The IPCC reports that some of the emissions of long-lived greenhouse gases stay in our atmosphere for several centuries after they are produced by whatever method. Global mean surface temperature increases and rising sea levels from thermal expansion of the ocean are projected to continue for hundreds of years after stabilization of greenhouse gas concentrations (even at present levels), owing to the long timescales on which the deep ocean adjusts to climate change. In other words, even if we produced zero CO_2 from this moment on, much of that which is already in the atmosphere would continue to pollute the atmosphere for hundreds of years into the future. This is why the fossil fuel dilemma and global warming are so closely connected.

How Much CO_2 in a Gallon of Gasoline?

A gallon of gasoline, which weighs 6.3 pounds, can produce twenty pounds of carbon dioxide (CO_2) when burned. Wow! Does that sound hard to believe? How can it be? Here's how. When

> *gasoline burns, the carbon combines with oxygen in the air to form carbon dioxide. How does that get to twenty pounds?*
>
> *Hold on to your socks. This gets complicated. Gasoline is 87 percent carbon and only 13 percent hydrogen. Thus 6.3 lbs of gasoline × 87 percent = 5.48 lbs of carbon per gallon. A carbon atom has an atomic weight of 12, and each of the two oxygen atoms has an atomic weight of 16. This means each CO_2 molecule has an atomic weight of 44 (12 from the carbon and 32 from the oxygen). The ratio of the carbon's molecular weight in CO_2 to the total weight of it in the gallon of gas is 12/44 or 0.27 (27 percent). This can be expressed as 27 percent of the CO_2 in the gas = 5.48 lbs. Solving for 100 percent, the weight of carbon in a gallon of gas is CO_2 = 5.48/0.27 = 20.3 lbs.*

Fossil fuels don't cause pollution in the atmosphere until we burn them. The faster that they are replaced with alternatives, the better off we will be in terms of air pollution. Many health-related problems are the direct result of burning fossil fuels like coal, and the air pollution they cause. We still need some kind of nonpolluting energies to replace them. The message is clear. Switching to clean burning alternatives helps keep our atmosphere clean and helps us to eliminate fossil fuel emissions from our lives.

The unfortunate truth about atmospheric pollution is that it respects no national barriers. The pollution generated in China shows up a few days later on our west coast. The burning of coal is one of the main causes of CO_2 and other toxic chemicals in our atmosphere, followed closely by automobile emissions. A major contributing factor to CO_2 is the rapid destruction of forests in places like Brazil and Africa. Some sources of greenhouse gases are more insidious and less obvious. Methane comes from some unlikely sounding places. It is generated in decaying garbage in our landfills, in swamps where organic material decays, and in cattle feeder lots from cow flatulence. Get your thinking caps on. Anyone with a solution to the latter problem can become an overnight billionaire.

The melting of the Arctic and Antarctic polar ice caps is stark physical evidence that our atmosphere is warming. It appears to be happening much faster than what was predicted too. Just recently (02/06/2009) an AP article reported that sea levels may be rising much faster than was predicted. It is theorized that when the ice melts off of the land, the removal of the enormous weight allows the land to rebound to higher levels. As that land rises above the ocean, it causes water levels to rise in other areas.

Arctic ice has been receding at a rate of 3 to 4 percent per decade. Since 2000, the rate of melting has accelerated to 8 percent per decade. Within ten years the Northwest Passage could be ice free for a month each year, permitting shipping to negotiate the passage without the use of ice breakers. The Northwest Passage reduces the shipping distance from Rotterdam to Yokohama by 4,700 miles resulting in significant savings in time, fuel, and Panama Canal fees.

The freeing of the Arctic Ocean from ice is beginning to cause some interesting international concerns. Prior to the melting, no one was ever concerned about who controls the Arctic, which has never belonged to any one country. Now many countries want to stake a claim, in part because it is thought that there are many important resources there, including oil. Russia has gone so far as to plant a flag on the Arctic Ocean floor.

Global warming is seen in changes of animal habitats, such as that of polar bears and penguins. Spring comes earlier and fall lasts longer. Hurricanes are more destructive, droughts more severe, floods more damaging, winters colder, and summers hotter. Ironically, global warming can cause colder winters in some areas because of changing weather patterns. Weather has become very erratic and unpredictable. Changes in the atmosphere are causing extinction of animal species to increase more rapidly.

There are few things we can do about the buildup of CO_2. Capturing it as it is produced at the smoke stack is possible, although expensive. Once captured, the question becomes, what can be done with it. One idea is to turn it into a liquid and pump it into depleted oil wells or porous rock strata and seal it into the ground. Scientists are not certain whether it will stay sealed in the ground or leak out, rendering our efforts futile and contributing to more pollution.

Another idea is to pump the CO_2 to the bottom of the ocean where the water is very cold keeping it on the bottom. Warm water rises and cold water sinks naturally. Again it is not known whether it will stay there. The ocean absorbs CO_2 from the air when it is cool making the water more acidic, and releasing it when it warms. Adding more CO_2 to the oceans kills coral by dissolving it with the carbonic acid resulting from mixing CO_2 with water. Coral beds are the nurseries for many kinds of fish. Killing the reefs will result in a reduction of fish populations. Many people the world over depend on fish for food.

There may be a way to combine CO_2 with magnesium turning it into magnesium carbonate to contain it. Other, so far unproven, technologies include biological systems taking advantage of genetically engineered plants to absorb CO_2. Nature provided us a wonderfully simple way to get rid of CO_2. They're called trees. Trees naturally absorb CO_2 and in return release oxygen through photosynthesis.

Our best, most immediate, and most reliable option is simply not to produce CO_2. In view of our current and increasing consumption of fossil fuels and projected growth, we will not be able to catch up with CO_2 production and head off global warming. Clearly we need fuels that produce zero pollution of any kind.

Cap and Trade

A system of limiting carbon emissions, called "cap and trade," is being proposed by the new U.S. administration. A cap would be placed on emissions. Under the CAP system, companies that exceed the allowed cap are able to buy credits from those who emit less than their allotted cap, thereby trading their emissions to a cleaner company. An alternative to this system might be an outright tax on all emissions, as an incentive to use less fossil fuel and reduce emissions.

CHAPTER 3: WHAT ARE ALTERNATIVE ENERGIES?

The easiest way to describe alternative energies is by the process of elimination. They are pretty much everything but fossil fuels. There are some qualifications, however, which need to be met. The following list presents a formidable set of qualifications that won't easily be met. They are as follows:

- Fuels should be renewable. This means that the source either replaces itself through growth, like plants, or is made from something of great abundance like sea water, oxygen in the air, or hydrogen that occurs in many organic compounds and it will be unlikely to ever run out.

- They should contain an energy density equal to or greater than that which they are meant to replace. Energy density means that it contains a high amount of energy per given volume. Gasoline and oil are the measure of high energy density. As an example, corn ethanol is a fairly low-density fuel and can't power big trucks or other heavy machinery.

- The cost of production, distribution, and storage should be equal to or less than that which it is meant to replace. Gasoline and oil have been relatively cheap to produce, store, and distribute, and the facilities for handling them are common throughout the country. They are our yardstick.

- They must be produced in a secure place not under the control of other governments. Ideally, they would be produced in the country in which they are to be consumed.

- Ideally, they must be available from continuous, noninterruptible means of production. Solar and wind energies are intermittent, but when paired with other acceptable alternatives, could be excellent choices for clean, nonpolluting alternatives. Storage is currently lacking for these alternatives, but researchers are hard at work on new types of energy storage.

- They should be nonpolluting, preferably producing no CO_2 or other greenhouse gases when burned, mined, or manufactured.

- They must not create any kind of hazardous waste materials that are costly to dispose of. Some suggested alternatives, like nuclear, do not meet this criteria, although research is currently ongoing to develop ways to recycle nuclear waste.

- They must not create competition for land or products that are universally used as food, taking food production out of the market. Ethanol from corn is not really a sustainable alternative because it takes so much energy and water to produce it, but ethanol can be made from other more efficient sources, such as grasses, wood waste, or algae. It should, however, be nonpolluting in manufacture or when burned. Ethanol is an acceptable alternative for interim use.

The list of alternatives presented and discussed in these pages is not meant to be the last word in alternatives, but is merely a snapshot in time of those most often discussed in the news media at the time of writing. Others will undoubtedly be discovered, proposed, and developed between now and the time we will need them as our primary sources of energy. It needs to be said that there probably won't be a single alternative that will fill all of our needs, but more likely a menu of several fuels that are best suited to different uses.

Alternative Fuels

1. Wind generation of electricity
2. Solar generation of electricity: photovoltaic solar
3. Passive solar heating: buildings designed as solar collectors

4. Focusing or concentrating solar heat and electrical generation

5. Other solar uses: Water heating, cooking, and lighting

6. Geothermal electricity generation

7. Geothermal: ground source heating and cooling

8. Hydroelectric generation: using the power of moving water

9. Tidal and wave energy generation of electricity

10. Biomass energy: making fuel from plants

11. Hydrogen: the universe's most plentiful fuel

12. Fuel cells: making electricity from hydrogen

13. Nuclear generation of electricity

The Smart Grid

The benefits of most of the electricity generating alternatives listed herein cannot be realized unless one vital step is taken first. We absolutely must build a new electric grid, and the grid must be smart, meaning it must be able to monitor the supply from multiple sources to control the generation, distribution, and consumption of power to everyone in the country. It must be able to ensure an uninterruptible supply to everyone, minimizing duplication and waste of our precious resources.

Our power grid developed in the early days of electrification as power companies were built. It is a patchwork system, and power failures are common. According to Thomas Friedman in his book, *Hot, Flat and Crowded,* if the grid was our highway system, it would be like driving across the country on country roads. The old dumb grid got its power from one source. The new smart grid will draw from multiple sources: wind, solar, geothermal, hydro, and even from solar collectors on our roofs.

The smart grid would be somewhat like the phone system, able to send the signal to anyplace in the country seamlessly. They keep records of our usage and can offer a cafeteria of plans depending upon our usage, time of day when we call, how many phones we have, and where we call to. The smart power grid will offer a variety of plans, monitor the time of day we use the most power, and charge us accordingly. It could do a great deal more, saving money and evening out loads, lessening the need for plants to be built just for a few days of the year when we have heaviest use. Our electrical appliances should be equally smart, running only when needed, sensing when we are home and when we are not. They should be able to communicate with the grid so that the demand for power is maintained at an optimum level, reducing the need for standby power generation.

CHAPTER 4: WIND ENERGY

Wind generation is a rapidly growing technology. It can and has been used for residential energy generation, particularly in remote areas where transmission lines are not available. The earliest use of wind power was in sailboats in Egypt about 4,000 BC. Windmills were in use in Iraq and Persia as early as the seventh century. The concept was brought back to Europe by the crusaders. Farms have used windmills for hundreds of years to pump water from wells and to grind grain. The Dutch put them to work to keep the ocean at bay by pumping water from low lands. Only in recent times have windmills been used to harness the wind for large-scale electricity generation.

Wind turbines are machines for generating electricity. The most common type resembling giant propellors usually have to be elevated to heights of one hundred feet or more to catch the prevailing winds and avoid turbulence caused by buildings and trees. They tend to be very imposing structures because the larger they are, the more efficiently they perform. Their size and the noise that they generate often cause opposition to their use near homes. There is also concern by wildlife advocates regarding bird kills. The largest ones turn slowly, transforming the energy by means of gears to ramp up the turbine speed. Wind energy from a turbine can be intermittent because the wind does not always blow with sufficient strength. At such times, stored or supplemental energy is required.

Disadvantages of Wind Turbines

Neighbors or homeowners' associations often consider proposed wind energy projects an eyesore, spoiling the landscape. Not everyone sees beauty in those highly visible, gently revolving, giant fan blades. Residential turbines of a size adequate to fully supply a home's energy needs are typically mounted on 80 to 100 feet high towers and produce 1.5 kWh. This is not normally enough to power the typical residence. Wind speeds must be above 8 to 10 mph for the blades to begin to revolve and generate electricity, although new turbine designs may overcome the speed requirement by functioning at lower wind speeds. Not only might neighbors object to those high towers, but local governments may also have prohibitions against them. There may also be ordinances against high structures of any kind in residential neighborhoods. In most places, building permits are required to construct a wind generator.

Horizontal Axis Wind Turbine

Even when there is sufficient land for such structures, problems have arisen. In a rural area North of Phoenix, Arizona, a wind turbine, approved by the local zoning board and well under way in construction on a ninety-seven-acre property, was appealed by area residents who claimed that the structure would be an eyesore and reduce their property values by spoiling their view. The world is full of contentious neighbors who are willing to take you to court over the design or height of your fence, or anything else that they may consider out of the ordinary. Arizona has a law that prohibits anyone from interfering with the installation of an energy-saving, renewable energy device, but it is not known if this has been tested in the courts yet. Several states have such ordinances.

To appease wildlife advocates, bird-friendly blade types are also being researched.

A residential wind turbine could lower your utility requirements 50 to 90 percent in areas with strong, constant winds. The exact amount depends upon the turbine's size, and the amount of electricity you use, the average local wind speed, obstructions, and other factors. A residential size wind turbine can cost anywhere from $22,000 to $46,000 installed. Commercial utility grade turbines that serve hundreds of homes can cost several million dollars apiece. Residential size wind turbines will generally recover their investment within six to fifteen years. Tax credits are available for wind energy electrical generation if the obstacles of size, appearance, and noise can be overcome. One can also sell power back to the power company with a wind turbine if it produces more than is consumed.

Wind Generation Case Study—The Maple Ridge Project

In upstate New York, in 2006, an area called the Tughill Plateau became the focus of a project called the Maple Ridge Wind Project. Constant winds sweep down from Lake Ontario, making it a prime location for wind generation. The project is now jointly owned by a Spanish company and Houston-based Horizon Wind Energy LLC. The latter is owned by Portuguese conglomerate Energias de Portugal. It is interesting to note that this project was conceived and built by foreign companies. At that time, European countries were ahead of the United States in the development of wind generation. However, in 2008 the United States surpassed all other countries becoming the largest user of wind generation.

The Maple Ridge Wind Project placed 195 four-hundred-foot-high wind turbines with 130 foot-long blades across the Tughill countryside. The turbines generate enough electricity to power one hundred thousand homes. To this farming community, the project brought new job opportunities. The cost to the developers was $400 million.

Landowners are getting $6,600 per year from each turbine on their property. Some love it, and some hate it. It has resulted in splitting families where offspring were opposed to the turbines on land that they stood to inherit. It also turned neighbors who opposed the project into enemies of those who approved. Clearly wind turbines are controversial. From Associated Press article in the *Arizona Daily Star*, August 17, 2008. "Turbines Bring NY Village Prosperity, at a Price."

Wind turbines need to be where the wind is reasonably constant. For the ordinary homeowner in a typical closely spaced subdivision, wind turbines do not appear to be a good fit.

Farming the Wind

Wind farms are a viable part of the alternative energy solution, but as noted, there are problems and perceptions to overcome. Offshore wind farms are promising because much larger turbines can be used. Their gigantic rotor blades move much slower and are thus less of a danger to wildlife. The wind offshore is more constant and unobstructed by buildings or trees. Transporting the large turbine blades is also easier by water. Wind farms are environmentally clean because they do not pollute the land, the water, or the atmosphere.

To date, wind generation of electrical energy remains quite expensive. Until the cost comes down considerably, and the issues with height and danger to wildlife are resolved, wind energy probably will be developed as large utility company wind farms in remote places. Transmitting electric power great distances results in some power being lost before it gets to the consumer. It is ironic that the best places for wind generation are often far from population centers. Nonetheless, there is much attention focused on this technology because of its clean energy-generating potential. The plains states and the seashore have the greatest potential for wind generation. While other areas are a mixed bag, one could imagine wind turbines on top of high-rise office buildings in a windy city like Chicago.

New Developments in Wind Generation

August 26, 2008, the *New York Times* announced that the company, Public Service Enterprise Group LLC, a subsidiary of P.S.E.G Energy Holdings, is forming a joint venture with Michael Nakhamkin, a leader in the development of energy storage technology. The new company, Energy Storage & Power, will promote the use of compressed air for storage technologies to utilities and other power producers. Wind turbines will be used to compress air to be stored in tanks. The compressed air will be released to add energy during peak hours or to run the generators when the wind is not blowing. The concept is not new, but only two such facilities now exist, one in Germany and the other in Alabama. Several projects are being considered by related companies and even an Iowa municipality.

Is Wind the Solution?

Wind-generated electricity qualifies as a viable alternative energy source on several counts. First, it is a known technology that has withstood the test of time. Once the expensive turbines are paid for, it is cheap. This means that some type of subsidy is required to make start-up installations viable. In October 2008, a federal-level investment tax credit for qualified small wind turbines was passed. The tax credit is valued at $500/.5 kWh capacity for up to $4,000 and available for small and micro-wind turbines (up to 100 kW), including vertical-axis wind turbines, installed through 2016. People are beginning to blog about their wind turbines.

While all is not roses, the objections to the size and appearance of the turbines can be overcome by placing them in remote locations. To the cost must be added the cost of building a new, smart energy grid to distribute the power to population centers. Finally, the storage of power must be solved to carry over windless days. Perhaps the smart grid can answer this question by supplying energy from solar or other means when the wind does not blow.

The 2009 administration is promising to provide help to the development of all alternative energies. Wind will be one of the major players in the mix. More efficient generators and energy storage will mean a large portion of our power generation will be from wind. There are even ideas for mounting solar collectors on the wind turbine towers boosting the power generated from these structures.

As the population comes to realize that they are safer and economically better off with alternative energies, many resistances will dissolve of themselves. Major changes rarely come easy.

CHAPTER 5: SOLAR ENERGY

We have an alternative energy source that is out of this world, or is it? The sun shines on the earth every day sending us enormous amounts of free energy, day in and day out, forever. The power of the sun is immense, and it drives our weather and the ocean currents. Without it, all life would cease to exist. It makes sense to use it in as many ways that we can. We now have the means to make use of the sun's power to provide electricity for our homes, offices, and large buildings. Power generated at the place of use means a savings of energy, otherwise lost through line resistance in transmission.

Photovoltaic Solar

Energy from the sun can take several paths to supply us with cheap, clean energy that is free from any emissions. Photovoltaic (PV) electric generation is a major source of alternative energy and a rapidly growing industry. *Photo* means light and *voltaic* means electric, thus photovoltaic means electricity from light.

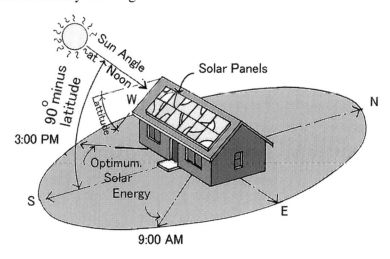

Solar Photovoltaic Principles

The best characteristic of solar energy is that the supply is inexhaustible. It is one of the top contenders of all the alternatives for home use. PV is attractive because of its modularity and flexibility. Solar panels can easily be configured to fit almost any roof with a south facing slope or a flat roof that will not be shaded by trees or other structures. If space permits, they can also be located on a spare piece of ground that will not be shaded. This is important because shade on even a small area of the solar panel can reduce the panel's effectiveness drastically.

Sun Angles Are Important

In the northern hemisphere, the ideal orientation for solar panels is facing due south, and inclined toward the sun at an angle equal to 90 degrees minus the latitude of your home's geographic location. This can vary depending on whether you want maximum electrical production in the morning or evening or in winter or summer. Solar PV panels can be equipped with computer-controlled tracking motors to keep them facing the sun for maximum efficiency. This is not common, and computer tracking does add considerably to the cost of PV systems. It is not essential for the collector panels to follow the sun, but it could boost efficiency by about 40 percent.

Solar PV systems can be quite costly, and the factors affecting cost need to be studied carefully before committing to installing a solar PV system. The tax credits and the opportunity to sell your energy back to the power company can reduce the cost significantly. Some power companies pay substantial incentives to homeowners who make their excess energy generation available to the power grid. Some states also have incentive programs. Check with your local utility company and your state Department of Energy.

How Does Solar Photovoltaic Work?

Think of your wireless, battery-free calculator on steroids, and you have a photovoltaic solar collector. The solar cells that make your calculator work are just like those that are used for solar collectors on your roof for generating electricity. Electric lights can actually generate a current to run your calculator, but sunlight is hundreds of times more powerful than artificial light. A module, such as you might find on a roof top collector, is simply a group of cells connected to one another and packaged together in a frame. Wires collect the electric current and take it to your electric meter and your house's electrical system.

Most photovoltaic cells are made of special materials called semiconductors, such as silicon, currently the most efficient and most commonly used. When light strikes the cell, the semiconductor material converts some of the light to electricity. By placing metal contacts at the top and bottom of the PV cell, the current can be drawn off into your home's electrical system, shunted to a battery backup system, or sent to the power company's energy grid. The main considerations that affect the cost of photovoltaic systems are the efficiency of the collector cells and the cost of manufacturing the collector panels. Most research is focused on increasing the efficiency of the collectors and finding collector materials that are not as expensive as silicon. Silicon cells are currently about 25 percent efficient. This needs to be increased to make them more affordable. Research has shown that if the face of the collector panel is nonreflective, more light is captured instead of being bounced back out, significantly increasing the collector's efficiency.

What Happens at Night?

Solar collectors of a sufficient size can generate all of the electricity needs for an average home, except of course at night. An array of panels two hundred square feet in size can generate about 2 kWh of power, enough for a house of about two thousand square feet. Since no sun is available for generation at night or on cloudy days, and there will always be some cloudy days, staying connected to the power company grid is required. Batteries are currently the subject of much research, for powering automobiles instead of gasoline, as well as for backing up photovoltaic systems. Fuel cells could also be used as a backup to generate electricity to supplement photovoltaic systems at night and on cloudy days, but they are currently very expensive.

At this time in our history, you could do little to make yourself feel better than becoming totally energy independent. It will become more feasible in the future as solar power generation comes down in price and storage for nighttime and cloudy days becomes more practical. Technological advances will undoubtedly result in more widespread use of photovoltaic generation of electricity in those parts of the country with adequate sunshine.

The Cost of Photovoltaic

The cost of installing a photovoltaic system on a home varies considerably, depending upon the size of the home and the power requirements of all the appliances, air conditioning, and other electronic devices to be connected. A small-sized system, designed to produce two thousand watts (two kilowatts), cost about $14,000 in 2008. That works out to $7 per watt installed. For a large residential system which is designed for a 5 kWh load, the installation cost could run $37,000 to $45,000, or $7.40 to $9.00 per watt. These figures are only important to tell you how much it will cost to install the collector and necessary equipment to get your system up and running. What you really want to know is how long it will take to pay that off. Right now those installation costs represent a serious investment. To put it in perspective, it is about what you would pay for a new car.

If your solar photovoltaic system is sized such that it can generate most of the electricity that you use, then your monthly utility costs will be negligible. The cost is determined by a net-metering system that consists of a second electric meter that the power company installs on your line. If you produce more electricity from the solar collectors than you are using at any given time, power will be sent back to the power grid, and the net meter will actually run backward.

Changes occurring from new legislation and from power company policies make this all a very dynamic process. Supposedly, at the end of the year, the power company nets out the electricity usage recorded by the meters and charges or pays you for the difference. Depending on policies and legislation, they may either reset your meter to zero or carry a credit forward into the next year. At the time of this writing, one can only state safely that you need to check with your power company or with an energy specialist whose job is to stay current on the rules.

The most popular information is that power companies must pay you for the energy you send into the grid at the "avoided" or wholesale cost in some locations and retail cost in others. Avoided cost is equal to the cost that the power company would have to pay to produce the same amount of energy themselves with coal or other fuels. The Arizona Consumer's guide to Buying Solar Electric Systems, produced by the U.S. Department of Energy, estimates the 2-kWh system could save 4,744 watts per year in Tucson, Arizona. At $0.08 per watt, that would be about $380 per year. Getting an exact estimate of savings depends on many variables, such as location, power company costs, your system size, and your normal usage.

Government Tax Credits and Rebates

Ideally one would draft a formula for calculating the payback period for installing a photovoltaic system, but it varies tremendously. There are new laws and policies almost daily, and the incentives vary from state to state. Individual usage patterns have an effect; power company rebates vary, and rates are dependent on location, time of day, and season. Estimating how long it would take to pay off the investment in a solar photovoltaic system is very difficult, but there is help out there.

Go to http://www.desire.usa.org and select your state on the site's map. This will bring you your state's Renewable Energy Credit Purchase Program, showing up-front incentives for all kinds of energy-saving systems, from solar, wind, and geothermal to biomass, natural lighting, and small hydroelectric. The site also lists sales tax exemptions, property tax exemptions, personal tax credits, permit fee credits, and efficiency incentives for single-family residences. To get a firm handle on what the cost and return on investment might be for a solar or other energy-saving system you might install, work with a competent, experienced contractor and your power company. Do not overlook how much an installed system might add to your home's appraised value. Some estimates place the increased value at around 25 percent.

Undoubtedly costs will come down in the future because of improvements in efficiency and competition in the market, making the payback period shorter. With power being produced at the place of usage, there is little loss due to line transmission. The power company wins because it reduces its need to build new plants, and the homeowner wins with cheaper electricity, and the United States wins by reducing its need for fossil fuel to generate electricity. The world wins because we have reduced air pollution. It is interesting to note that each kilowatt hour of electricity produced saves two pounds of carbon dioxide, one half gallon of water, and prevents emissions of nitrogen oxide, sulphur dioxide, and mercury.

Before installing a photovoltaic solar system, it is wise to consult an architect, engineer, or a competent supplier of system components with experience in the design and installation of PV systems. Even the siting of your house is very important. There are important considerations that the consultant will help you understand about your system's orientation and locality. You will want to maximize the effectiveness of your investment.

New Developments in Photovoltaic Energy

Photovoltaic Coatings

New developments in the field of photovoltaic energy have produced new PV coatings that can turn windows, and even roof surfaces, into PV collectors at a reasonable cost. The semitransparent coatings would allow windows to continue to function as windows. The longevity of these materials is currently too short, but research will continue and that shortcoming will hopefully be overcome in the future.

Innovations in the manufacture of solar cells are already promising lower prices approaching "grid parity," which is generally accepted as $1.00 per watt. In order to compete with coal-powered generation, the manufacturing cost would have to be around 60–70 percent of grid parity to give the solar panel manufacturer a reasonable profit. It is reasonable to assume that grid parity will eventually be achieved in the not too distant future, particularly with the tax credit program.

Photovoltaic Roofing

In the fall of 2008 *Technology Review*, published by Massachusetts Institute of Technology, announced that United Solar Ovonic of Auburn Hills, Michigan, has teamed with a major roofing company to create a metal roofing system that generates electricity from sunlight. The material is more aesthetic than regular rooftop mounted solar panels, and this enables the homeowner to avoid wrangles with opinionated neighbors or homeowners' associations. Since the solar collecting material is, in fact, the roofing material, it would save money if solar was added when roof replacement is needed or at the time of new construction. The material carries a twenty-year warranty. Neighbors should be happier with the appearance of integrated solar roofing. This assumes that the angles of an existing roof is suitable for solar collection.

New Photovoltaic Collector Designs

An MIT researcher has discovered how to make cells 50 percent more efficient by making them multilayered thus trapping the light in the collector longer instead of bouncing it back into space. They also added an antireflective coating on the face of the collector to aid in trapping the light that is usually bounced off.

The price of solar cells based on silicon wafers currently fluctuates around $3 to $4 per watt. The demand right now has created a shortage of silicon, but by the end of 2010, the shortage should be over and prices should drop substantially.

One company has developed cells using glass panels instead of the more expensive silicon. They are only about 10 percent efficient while silicon cells can achieve about 25 percent efficiency. It is expected that the glass panel system will achieve 12 percent efficiency soon, but that is still quite low.

Focusing systems that track the sun are much more efficient than regular flat collector panels. They are also currently much more expensive. Until the price of collectors with sun-tracking equipment comes down, focusing systems would be more costly to install than a flat panel system.

Photovoltaic systems are easily adapted to existing houses as well as new homes although roof angles or tree shade can present problems. Even apartment buildings could utilize photovoltaic collectors to supply some of the apartment complex's power needs.

Some PV cells work best in sunny warm climates like the southwestern states, where up to three hundred days of sun per year are possible. Other types will work anywhere. In most cases, the more sun that is available the better a PV system will work. It is worth noting that a University of Arizona researcher has discovered that in the desert, solar panels can overheat and cause a reduction in efficiency. These environmental considerations should be studied to determine the feasibility of each alternative for your locality.

The National Energy Research Laboratory (NERL) is experimenting with several types of solar-collecting systems, including arrays of small focusing solar dishes for photovoltaic generation. The tracking of the sun's path and the utilization of focusing dish collectors double the efficiency of the collector. See http://www1.eere.energy.gov/solar/index.html.

A Promising Alternative

At this time, solar photovoltaic holds the most promise for alternative energy that can be used directly by the homeowner, depending on location. Almost daily, technological advances in the manufacture of PV cells are bringing the cost down and increasing efficiency. Suddenly, with the new 2009 tax incentives, PV power generation has just become much more affordable. All of these new developments will make solar PV an attractive alternative to oil or coal for generating electricity. If you live in an area that gets more than average sunshine over the year, and you do not mind a reasonable wait for your investment to show a return, then solar photovoltaic is a good option. A major benefit of placing solar collectors on or near the customer's house is in the efficiency of energy transmission, placing no load on the grid except for sunless periods and at night.

The reality is that photovoltaic electric power generation is not cheap, even with the governmental incentives, and represents a major investment that not everyone can afford. For those folks, ideas are afloat to have power companies pay for the investment to put solar systems onto homes. Other private companies are now offering such arrangements. You would pay the private installer a monthly fee, and the company would deal with the utility. The equipment can be leased, and the homeowner pays monthly, just like the electric bill. Leasing could overcome the large initial investment. It could possibly be a lease to own type arrangement, where the homeowner eventually buys the system.

Finally, if you are a handy DIY person, there are places to get help installing your own photovoltaic collector system, thereby reducing the cost of a system considerably. A company called Real Goods in Boulder, Colorado, sells helpful books and lots of information on installing a solar system, including all of the equipment you would need: collector panels and inverters and lots of other green living items. They have wind turbines too. Go to http://www.realgoods.com.

A Photovoltaic Case Study

If there is any place in the United States that is right for solar photovoltaic generation of electricity, it is Tucson, Arizona. Tucson gets, on average, three hundred days of sunshine a year. Tucson architect Rosemary Latshaw was engaged by a Tucson doctor and his wife to design an addition to their existing 3,325-square-foot home. The couple wanted to add a photovoltaic solar system for the entire house. The addition was to be a guest/study of 680 square feet plus a single car garage, and this brought the total area of the house to 4,005 square feet.

Dealing with Homeowners' Associations and Neighbors

A Homeowner Association (HOA) can be difficult to deal with, and for the doctor and his wife, this project proved to be no exception. It took three tries to get approval for their plan. The original plan was to mount the solar panels at the correct angle on the flat roof of the new guest room, but obscure them from ground level with a raised eighteen-inch parapet wall around the flat roof. The HOA insisted that the flat roof on the guest/study be changed to match the south sloping roofline of the existing house. The owners complied despite the fact this change was neither an esthetic improvement to the existing house nor the addition.

The neighbors, whose home is adjacent to the addition on the south side, made it very clear that they did not want to look at the solar panels, even on a sloping roof. Their wishes were honored, so no solar panels were placed on the roof of the guest/study portion of the addition. This meant that twelve panels had to be omitted from the project, reducing the system's capacity by a third. In spite of these obstacles, the owners still were able to reduce their electrical bills substantially. The twelve omitted panels could well have allowed them to generate most, if not all, of their daytime electrical requirements. The law was on the side of the energy conscious couple, but they were also people who wanted to live in peace with their neighbors, so they eliminated the twelve panels. Nevertheless, homeowners' associations, neighborhoods, and even individuals need to come to grips with the energy problems we face in this country. We have to change our way of thinking, and it is fair to say that in most cases, old ideas and habits die hard.

The Homeowners' Association and the neighbors' objections illustrate what can happen when doing something with your own property does not fit the norm of your neighborhood, or your neighbor's ideas about what your home should look like. The doctor and his family might have been able to persevere if they had chosen to fight it, because it is against the law in Arizona to interfere with the installation of systems that save energy. However, it could have resulted in a legal battle, making the installation very costly.

Solar Panels on Garage

The cost of this installation is considerably less than it would have been without the rebates from the power company. Power companies are mandated to generate a small percentage of their electricity from renewable energy. This has created a market in credits for doing so, which was likely one reason that they would be generous in handing out rebates. These credits have value and may be bought by another utility company that is subject to a Renewable Portfolio Standard or by a broker who deals in public utilities. Because Tucson has a warm winter climate and gets on average three hundred days of sunshine per year, the power company could expect to gain power for the grid at times when the family's heating and cooling needs are not high. Those in other parts of the country will get different results from those that this family got. In turn, rebates will vary according to another company's expected energy return, given their location.

Twelve Solar Panels on Porch Roof

Had the solar PV system been installed when the house was built, and integrated into the house design, some of the HOA's and neighbors' objections might have been averted by altering the floor plan and locating the house differently on the site. It would also have made it easier to prepare the roof before the tile went on. Solar roofing could have also avoided problems of acceptance.

Chapter 6: Passive Solar

Passive solar is the term that describes a building designed such that it becomes a solar collector itself. The functionality of this type of building relies on most of its windows facing south to admit the sun's rays in the winter, and shading designed to block the rays in the summer, either with overhangs or some type of movable shading device. Reservoirs of water, masonry walls, and concrete floors can be used as a heat sink, or storage device, to catch and retain the heat in the living space, releasing it slowly at night.

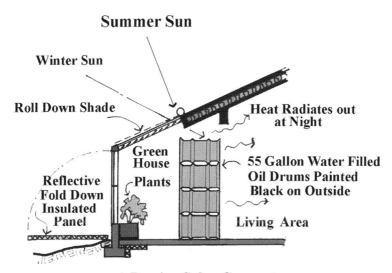

A Passive Solar Concept

Passive solar design can be adapted to any structure, but it must be an integral part of the design to take full advantage of its benefits. Some passive solar ideas can be adapted to existing homes, but it is most effective when incorporated into the original design. The beauty of passive solar is that it requires little in the way of mechanical equipment to heat the space and uses no fuel of any kind if properly designed and insulated, unless conditions require heat at night or for very cold days. Proper insulation for some very cold areas may exceed normal requirements for a nonpassive solar building so consultation with a design professional is recommended.

Passive Rules of Thumb

- The building should be elongated east to west to maximize the sun exposure on the south side.

- The building's south face should receive the sun's rays between 9:00 a.m. and 3:00 p.m. during the heating season.

- Those interior spaces requiring the most heating and lighting should be along the south face of the building.

- Spaces not occupied frequently, such as laundry rooms, furnace rooms, closets, and bathrooms, should be on the north.

- An open floor plan optimizes passive solar design by allowing the heat to freely circulate throughout, and helps provide natural light for spaces not adjacent to windows.

- Shading should be employed to keep the summer sun out of the interior, but allow it in during the heating season. Shading devices can be movable, using hinged or sliding panels or roll-up awnings, or they can be fixed with an overhang calculated to block summer sun but admit the winter sun.

- There must be ample south-facing glass, preferably of the double or triple insulating type.

- There must be some type of thermal mass to absorb, store, and distribute the heat. Uncarpeted floors of tile on concrete or stained and polished concrete make good thermal mass, as do masonry walls. The ideal thickness of the thermal mass is no more than six inches.

Knowing the Sun's Angles

Passive solar requires a thorough understanding of sun angles and movements during the different seasons. It relies on the ingenuity and knowledge of a skilled designer to take maximum advantage of the sun and other environmental factors, such as prevailing winds, terrain, and surrounding landscaping. Reducing or eliminating north-facing windows in a cold climate can make a tremendous difference on heating loads. Careful weather stripping of all doors and windows is essential because much of the heat loss or gain comes from around these openings. All areas where air can penetrate the building envelope, as well as areas exposed to the outside, must be caulked and insulated. Small openings can admit an amazing amount of cold air with a 20 mph wind. Upper floors that project beyond the lower story's outside walls should be carefully insulated as well as spaces adjacent to uninsulated attic spaces and garages.

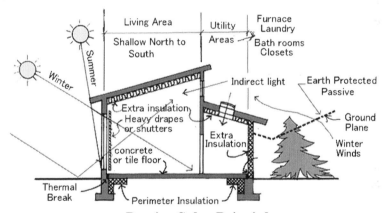

Passive Solar Principles

If you are building a new house, passive solar design should be at the top of your list of options, because it does not take a huge investment. Even with a photovoltaic system, passive solar concepts are helpful in reducing your energy requirements with little effort or expense. Some passive solar principles can be incorporated into any existing home, too. Ideally, in the future, all buildings will be designed with passive solar principles.

A company, previously mentioned in the section on photovoltaic, called Real Goods (www.realgoods.com) sells a passive solar collector, which warms the air inside a home. It can be installed in an existing home in a window or built into the walls of a new structure. Cool air enters the bottom of the panel, where it is heated, after which it exits at the top into the room interior. The window installation would, of course, blank out the window because the panel is solid black in color to maximize heat collection.

Earth Sheltered Passive

Earth-sheltered homes are a special case of passive solar and are possible in the vast majority of the continental United States. This involves either mounding earth up around the exterior walls or building the house into a south-facing hillside. Earth makes a good insulator and heat sink depending on the depth and thickness of the soil. The soil maintains a uniform outside temperature of about fifty-five degrees Fahrenheit below a depth of five feet year round, thus protecting the building envelope from wide temperature swings, lessening the heating and cooling load.

The main principle of passive solar design, or any type of construction for that matter, is to design the structure to maximize heat gain in the winter and minimize it in the summer. Earth-sheltered construction does this very well. If the roof is also earth covered, the earth covering should be at least six inches thick to even out the wide fluctuations in exterior temperature. Main heat loss or gain would be from any windows or wall surfaces exposed to the outside. The weight of earth on the roof must be considered in the structural member design, including the weight of water that would saturate the earth when it rains. Earth protection of the roof can also be accomplished with plants in shallow, closely spaced containers that can be removed in case of the need for roof repairs. Ground covers or shrubs planted on an earth mound can also help insulate the roof from heat gain or loss.

In a well-insulated earth-protected passive solar house, the temperature difference between a comfortable seventy-two degrees and the fifty-five-degree earth outside can easily be maintained by heat from cooking, appliances, lighting, and the heat sink walls and floors.

Natural ventilation can also be very effective in making any passive solar home more livable. This involves letting air in to a space low on an exterior wall and exhausting it high on an opposite wall, letting the natural tendency of hot air to rise to create a flow of air. Operable skylights or high windows will facilitate natural ventilation.

Chapter 7: Focusing Solar

Focusing or concentrating solar refers to systems that use parabolic reflectors to focus the sun's rays on a pipe, boiler, photovoltaic collector, or solar furnace. They are sometimes referred to as solar heat to differentiate them from photovoltaic. Parabolic refers to the shape of the mirrored collectors that focus the sun's rays like a spotlight or magnifying glass. Parabola is the geometrical term for the shape taken by a chain, rope, or cable suspended from each end and allowed to hang freely. A reflector in the shape of a parabola reflects the sun's rays to a focal point, the location of which depends on the shape of the reflector.

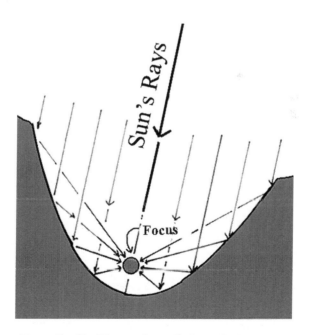

Parabolic Focusing Solar Collector

Parabolic collectors can be configured in two ways. One is a continuous parabolic trough, shown above, which focuses the sun's rays on a pipe located at the focal point running the length of the trough. The pipe contains a heat transfer medium, which is either oil or water. The pipe containing the heat transfer medium connects with multiple rows of identical collectors taking the hot oil or water to the generating plant to make steam, which turns the turbine generator. The second type is a series of dish-shaped parabolic collectors that all focus on a single point where the solar furnace or collector is located. This type can generate very intense heat that could melt steel pipes if they were not filled with water or oil. The dish type, because they are designed and computerized to follow the sun throughout the day, are highly efficient.

The sun's rays can heat the oil heat transfer medium to seven hundred degrees Celsius (1,292 degrees Fahrenheit). This super-heated oil is then used to turn water into steam. Steam can be generated by heating the water in a solar boiler directly, eliminating the need for the oil intermediate step, but steam tends to lose efficiency (heat) in the process of piping it to the turbine. The oil transfer medium is contained in a special double-walled pipe that maintains the extreme heat making it more efficient than a water transfer medium.

Focusing Solar Farms

Typically, focusing collectors are built in large arrays or groups by companies that generate and sell power that goes into thousands of homes. Focusing solar could be used in a residence for space and water heating, but it is not commonly used at this time because of the cost of the computerized equipment required. In the future, we might see focusing solar being developed for home electricity generation. Construction and operating costs preclude the use for an individual consumer at this time.

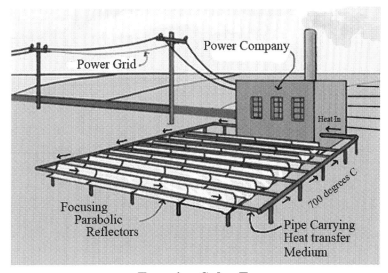

Focusing Solar Farm

Focusing Solar and Coal Combination

An article in MIT's *Technology Review*, February 10, 2009, "Cutting Coal Use with Sunshine," by Peter Fairley, reported on experiments with combining solar collectors with existing coal fired power-generating plants. The solar collectors feed heat into the plant at 400°C boosting the heat of the steam being heated by coal to 550°C making the plant more efficient. At night the gas or coal fuel takes over keeping the power generation going continuously. Placing the solar generating plant adjacent to an existing coal fired plant shares the daytime load without compromising the coal plant's capacity at night.

There are two important things to consider in placing solar collection fields near a power plant: collectors need a large area of land, and there is an energy loss in transmitting the solar energy back to the generating turbines if land isn't available nearby. A problem with either could add considerably to the cost of such an installation, as well as result in a reduction of efficiency. Many coal- or gas-fired generating plants may be located where the lack of sufficient, continuous sunshine makes a collection field impractical.

The purpose for developing paired solar/fossil fuel generating plants is to reduce CO_2 when the sun shines and fill in with fossil fuel power when the sun is not available. When a price is finally put on CO_2 production these facilities could become economically feasible. If used in connection with focusing solar collectors, coal-fired plants could achieve much greater reductions in CO_2 than gas-fired plants.

An Interesting Proposal

Currently there are visionary ideas being investigated worldwide by scientists in the field of solar energy. Some ideas are on a grand scale. For instance, the National Space Society (www.nss.org) is promoting space-based solar power, and it is not new. This has been under study since the 1970s. The plan suggests placing solar collectors in orbit around the earth and beaming the energy down wirelessly by microwave to collectors on earth's surface. Solar energy available in space is billions of times greater than all energy sources available on earth. Because the sun never sets in space and clouds cannot interfere, the potential is enormous. Wireless energy transmission from solar collectors to the earth by microwave is already a proven technology, although not to the scale needed to make this concept work.

As crazy as it sounds, you might ask why this might even be considered. Too far out? That may or may not be. Military scientists don't think so. They express concern that the dwindling energy resources now in use may cause future world wars. This will be increasingly apparent as world population expands. They indicate that space-based solar power could provide true energy independence to all nations, easing competition for scarce fossil fuels. As space technology improves, tapping this solar power may provide the means for a peaceful sharing of essential power.

The main disadvantage to space-based solar power is the cost of developing the system, and only governments will likely have the capital to pioneer the way. However, by way of perspective, waging wars over resources could be far more expensive than the cost of developing a space-based solar system. Scrambling to salvage property and relocate people resulting from global warming could be staggeringly expensive. If oceans and seas rise, building barriers to rising water will not be cheap. In its favor, space-based solar power utilizes mostly existing technologies. It takes advantage of our existing historic investment in space. It would create new industries and jobs.

Here's an idea that will boggle the mind. It could be that a cable, anchored in space by a satellite in synchronous orbit, could carry the satellite-collected power to earth. There are proposals being studied right now to place an elevator into space anchored to a satellite. While it takes time and technological advances to turn the unimaginable into the practical, these visionary efforts represent the type and scale of thinking required to replace our dependence on fossil fuels. Today's science fiction is tomorrow's science fact.

Some political questions that accompany a solution of this magnitude can affect the entire world. It is a project that would be best served by international planning, cooperation, and financing, but the time for this planning is now. The clock is ticking.

Chapter 8: Other Solar Uses

Solar Water Heating

Generating hot water is the second largest use of energy in American households after heating and cooling. Before considering solar water heating, you should make every effort to conserve hot water by wrapping the hot water tank with an insulating blanket, fixing those dripping faucet, using low-flow showerheads, and insulating your hot water pipes. Then, if you wish to pursue installing a solar water heater, you need to calculate the size and type that you need.

For a household of four, an eighty-gallon tank would produce twenty gallons per day per person. Multiply the number of persons to be served by twenty to arrive at your tank size. In the Sunbelt, use one square foot of collector for each two gallons of tank capacity for daily household usage.

- Sunbelt: An eighty-gallon tank would require 80 / 2 gallons = 40 sq. ft. of collector.

- Southeast and mountain states: 80 / 1.5 gallons = 53 sq. ft. of collector

- Midwest and Atlantic states: 80 / 1 gallon = 80 sq. ft.

- New England and Northwest: 80 / 0.75 gallons = 106.6 sq. ft.

Solar Batch Heaters

This is the simplest of all the solar water heater systems. The storage tank is placed on the roof, and the sun heats the water directly. Incoming cold water from the water main goes first to the heater on the roof. Note: the roof structure must be able to hold the weight of a tank full of water, which is substantial. No pumps are required because the hot water flows by thermal differential. Hot water rises and cold water drops. Water only flows to the house when it is used. Temperature and pressure relief valves are required because these systems can produce very hot water. It is desirable to add a manual bypass valve system that will allow you to bypass the regular water heater in summer when the solar system is doing the job by itself. These systems should only be used where it never freezes in winter.

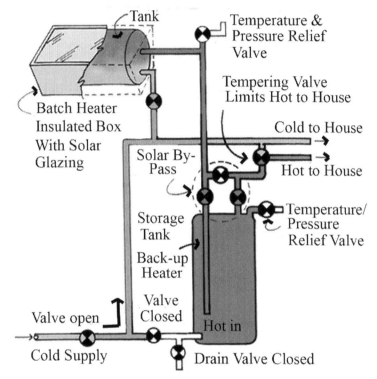

Solar Batch Water Heater

An improvement on this design would be to separate the collector from the storage tank, bringing the storage tank into a warm area so that stored heat would not be lost to the night sky. It takes all day to heat the whole tank, but if you separate the collector and tank, you can increase the collector size, insulate the storage tank better, and get hot water much sooner. In this case, the incoming water can be pumped to the collector, consisting of water-filled tubes, and the regular water heater becomes the storage tank. There are several variations on this type of solar water heater system. Check with local installers for the type best suited for your area.

Closed-Loop Water Heater

A closed-loop heat exchanger is the most reliable protection from freezing and bursting the pipes. In this type of system, an antifreeze solution is circulated from the collector on the roof to the storage tank in a closed system, heating the water with a coil in the storage tank. The house water and antifreeze never mix. These closed loop systems have more parts and are consequently more expensive. They have a high degree of reliability and are well understood by most heating contractors.

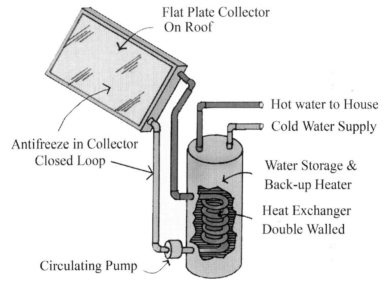

Closed-Loop Solar Water Heater

Drain-Back or Draw-Down Water Heater

This is a simpler version of the closed-loop system. The collector uses water in the collector instead of antifreeze, and when the system is not in operation, the water drains back down to a storage tank in a warm area.

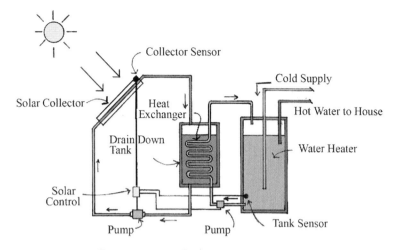

Draw Down Solar Water Heater

Draw-Down or Drain-Back Solar Water Heater

Open-loop systems are subject to problems from corrosion unless corrosion-resistant materials are used, like copper, bronze, brass, stainless steel, plastic, and glass lining for hot water tanks. This increases the cost. Closed systems exclude oxygen, the main culprit in corrosion of metal parts. Solar water heaters cost between $3,500 and $4,500. For new construction, the cost could be amortized over the period of your loan, usually twenty to thirty years. Systems can also be installed in existing homes saving approximately half of your water heating bill. There are federal tax credits for installing solar water heaters too.

More Solar Uses

Solar Swimming Pool Heating

Pool heaters are very effective in extending the swimming season, depending upon the part of the country in which you live. They function much the same way that a solar water heater does, except the reservoir is your swimming pool. The temperature of a typical residential pool can be raised six to eight degrees Fahrenheit in a single day with a solar system and maintain it even on partly cloudy days. If an insulating plastic bubble type pool cover is used, the heat is maintained over cool nights. They are typically made with trapped air bubbles like bubble wrap, which acts as an insulating blanket. Since they are made of petroleum they are not necessarily an energy friendly solution, but they do reduce evaporation and conserve water as well as heat. Depending upon your location, the heaviest type of insulating pool cover may last two or more years. For a 20ft × 35ft pool they would cost about $225. If you have an irregular pool shape, simply use a pair of scissors to cut it to fit. The insulating blanket can increase pool temperature considerably by itself, but the solar coil heater can raise temperature much more rapidly, particularly during the shoulder season while the sun's angle is low.

Black Plastic Coil Pool Heater

The simplest and least expensive type of pool heater utilizes black plastic pipe coils placed on the roof or the ground that are connected to the regular pool pump. If your home is two stories, the pump size may have to be increased in size to lift the water to the roof. This system is best for a single-story flat roof or ground-level installation due to their appearance and the difficulty attaching them to a sloping roof. Normally they can simply lie directly on the roof and are easily removed for roof maintenance. If your roof is sloping, you should consider the panel collectors, which would be attached to the roof.

Sensors are located on the roof and on the return line from the pool to the pump. When the incoming water from the pool falls below the temperature at which you have set the thermostat, a valve opens to bring water from the collector. When the water reaches the set temperature, the valve will automatically close or open to maintain that temperature.

It requires piping to and from the roof and the automatic valve and controls, and a connection to the incoming pool water. The average installation costs of the plastic coil system are approximately $2,000 for a pool that holds twenty thousand gallons of water. Heating a pool in cool weather with a gas heater can cost several hundred dollars just for the initial heat up, and maintaining it for any length of time can increase your gas bill at a rate that makes you gasp. Depending upon the cost of gas, the solar system would soon pay for itself, very likely within a year.

Solar Cooking

Solar cooking has been around for a long time. The author used a simple solar oven back in the 1940s to bake biscuits on Boy Scout camping trips. They can be used to cook virtually anything. They heat rapidly and are easy to use. A solar oven is a shallow, insulated box with a transparent glass or plastic cover to trap the heat. The inside surfaces are shiny to reflect the heat. There is usually a black metal cooking surface on the bottom, raised on pedestals to reduce the transmission of heat through the bottom of the box. External reflective flaps can be added on one or more sides, made of reflective metal or wood or cardboard covered with aluminum foil, shiny side out. The flaps, like those on an open cardboard packing box, help reflect the sun into the box. Some commercial solar ovens are so large as to require a trailer to haul them around. The suitcase size ovens are easily transportable and are being used by campers, hunters, and in developing countries to cook, purify water, or sterilize surgical instruments. They can also be used to dry and preserve fish or fruit. Commercially made solar ovens are readily available on the Internet. The homeowner can use a solar oven in lieu of a gas or charcoal grill, and it emits no pollution, except when you burn the burgers. A small solar commercial oven, made of metal about two feet square in size, can be purchased for about $300.

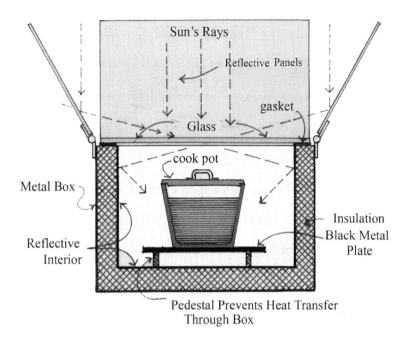

Solar Box Oven

Skylights

Skylights were probably the first use of solar energy for lighting. They are still used and are popular because of the amount of light they can bring to the interior of buildings in the daytime. They should always be double glazed or triple glazed to reduce the heat gain and loss, and should not be larger than 10 percent of the interior space in which they are used. Double and triple glazing reduces the heat transfer, but it is still substantial. If used in conjunction with some type of translucent shading or integral Venetian blinds between the glass panels, heat gain can be substantially reduced. Skylights can then be used shaded in summer for the light they provide and unshaded in winter for passive solar heating. Double-glazed skylight products include Energy Star skylights that have nonconductive framing, are double glazed with an air or gas sandwich, and use Low-E glass with special coatings. Energy Star skylights are eligible for federal tax credits. Some states also give tax credits for these energy-efficient skylights. Operable skylights can be opened for cross ventilation to increase comfort in summer.

Light Pipes

Light pipes were the next generation of solar lighting. They consist of metal tubes with a reflective interior and a clear dome at the roof that bounces the sun's rays down into the interior. Some have lenses that aid in reflecting the light downward. They appear similar to regular ceiling lights and can be controlled to some extent by dimming. They are reasonably inexpensive to install and are very effective for bringing natural light to a dark corner. They can even pass through an attic and still be effective as a light fixture. These can be used where space or structure prohibits skylights.

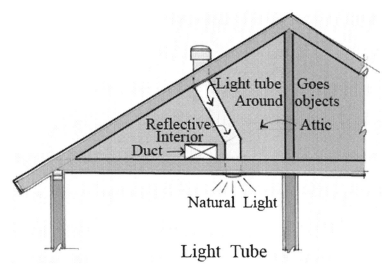

Solar Light Pipe

Hybrid Solar Lighting

The latest development in solar lighting is a cross between solar and regular wired electric lights. The hybrid solar light pipes bring light from the roof by fiber optics. A sensor balances the solar light with the electric light to maintain an even level, depending upon the available sun. The fixture would be totally electric at night and on dark cloudy days. Fiber optics uses the same technology that transmits data and phone conservations through glass fibers. It is currently undergoing testing at the Oak Ridge National Laboratory in collaboration with the Department of Energy.

There are undoubtedly other uses for solar collection being developed momentarily. The possibilities are nearly endless. Solar could be used to power fuel cells to be used as a backup system at night and on cloudy days. The cells can be used for virtually anything and everything that uses electric power. Nearly everything that now runs on wired electricity could be made to work on solar collection over time. The only caveat is that if a device needs power at night or on cloudy days, it will need a backup battery, fuel cell, or other source of power.

Chapter 9: Geothermal Energy

There are two types of geothermal energy. The first and most often thought of as geothermal is the natural heat from the earth's molten interior. Water is piped into the super heated rock strata, producing very hot water or steam, which can be used to turn a turbine and generate electricity. Cooler, but also very hot water can be used for space heating, aquaculture, snow melting, food processing, dehydration, hot tubs, and spas.

Geothermal Generation of Electricity

If you have ever been to Yellowstone Park, you have seen the first type of natural geothermal energy in action. Ground water seeps into cracks in the earth's crust, where it is heated until it becomes steam. The force of the expanding steam forces the incoming water up through the earth's crust, and we have a geyser like Old Faithful.

The first geothermal power plant in the United States was at the Geysers in California. It was opened in 1960 and is still operating successfully. California is the leader in the U.S. production of electricity from geothermal energy, but they may soon be eclipsed by Alaska. State officials have announced recently that they are funding exploration and surveying of Alaska's largest volcanoes with the intent of providing energy to power thousands of homes. Estimates are that these volcanoes and hot springs can supply up to 25 percent of the state's energy needs.

Geothermal power plants, most of which are concentrated in the western United States, provide the third largest domestic source of renewable energy. While they provide less than 1 percent of the United States' electrical power now, they have the potential to provide over 20 percent of national needs. If one lives in an area of geothermal activity, geothermal can be a good source of energy, although private use by an individual homeowner is generally not a choice. Most of us are not blessed with a hot spring in our backyard. For large power plants, however, it can certainly provide an inexhaustible source of energy with no accompanying pollution.

As of May 2007, geothermal electric power was generated in five U.S. states. According to the Geothermal Energy Association's recent report, there were also seventy-five new geothermal power projects underway in twelve states as of that date.

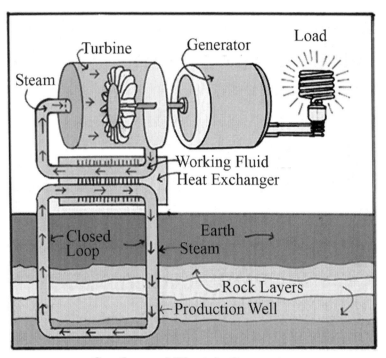

Geothermal Electric Generator

Geothermal wells can be drilled in areas where hot water does not find its way to the surface naturally. Deep wells can be drilled, much like an oil well, down to the level where heat from the earth's molten core can be tapped. Water is then pumped down the hole through a closed loop of pipes. The water circulating back up is heated and can be used for electrical generation, space heating, or water heating. The problem with this process is that eventually the water cools the rock, and new wells must be drilled after about five years.

Geothermal or Ground Source Heat Pumps

The second type of geothermal energy, referred to as geothermal or ground source heat pumps, uses the constant temperature of the earth as a means of heating or cooling the refrigerant of a typical heat pump. Holes or trenches are dug, into which pipes are installed for circulating water. The water is cooled or heated by the constant fifty-five degrees Fahrenheit of the earth, which results from the sun's heat being absorbed by the earth. The refrigerant gas is heated to fifty-five degrees by the water from the ground loop and then compressed, causing it to be heated to the desired temperature. When it returns to the heat pump, it expands causing it to cool, a process that can be used for cooling or be reversed for heating.

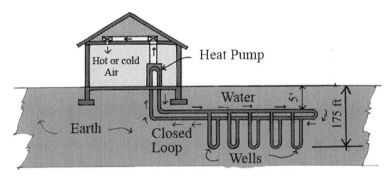

Ground Source Geothermal Heat Pump

Geothermal heat pumps can be used almost anywhere in the temperate zones of the continental United States. The buried water lines, which are the heart of the geothermal heat pump, can take different configurations, depending upon soil conditions and the amount of area available for burial. Lines can be buried vertically in a drilled hole or laid horizontally in four- to five-feet-deep trenches and spread out as space permits. Heat pumps can also be used by placing a closed water-filled loop below the surface of a lake or pond. If a pond or lake is used, the water should be at least eight feet deep in cold climates to prevent the pipes from freezing. A closed-loop design should be used to transfer the heat to and from the water; otherwise, wildlife such as crawfish or mussels can clog the intake pipe, rendering the system inoperable.

Geothermal heat pumps operate on the same basic principles as air-to-air heat pumps, but air-to-air heat pumps are much less efficient because of the fluctuations in the outside air temperatures. In both types, some kind of supplemental heat is usually required in colder climates where the temperature falls below forty degrees Fahrenheit. Electric resistance heating is most often used. Resistance heating is what browns your toast in the toaster. Electricity heats wires to where they radiate intense heat. Electric resistance heating can be quite expensive in cold climates. In addition to electric resistance heating, heat pumps require power to run the compressor and fans that move the air over the heating/cooling coils. This power could be supplied by renewable sources such as photovoltaic, wind, or fuel cells.

A Geothermal Heat Pump Retrofit—A Case Study

In May of 2007, John Kemper, an architect living in St. Louis, purchased a three-story brick house built in 1930. It had a hot water heating system with radiators and no central air conditioning. His goal was to add air conditioning and to reduce the cost of heating his home. He considered photovoltaic solar, but St. Louis doesn't get a lot of sunshine in the winter. He added to the original insulation in the attic, which was minimal, rewired the house, and installed ductwork from the heat pump unit's air handler.

To design the geothermal system, he hired a heating and cooling contractor. Although he personally designed the configuration of the duct system, he worked with the contractor for placement of the registers, transfer ducts, and return air grilles. The project took four months but could have been completed faster, except for the other renovation work being done concurrently.

The entire system cost around $40,000 including ductwork, which the original house never had. He was eligible for an unfunded Section 412 of the federal Energy Independence and Security Act of 2007, which offered incentives for geo-exchange. It promised a 25 percent rebate (up to $3000) for expenditures to install a renewable energy system. There were no rebates available from the gas or electric company. At the time of writing, he had not received the federal incentives.

Seven vertical wells, 175 feet deep, are connected in a loop and then to two heat pump units in the basement. A pump circulates water in that loop when there is a demand for heating or cooling, delivering a constant flow of fifty-five-degree water to the heat pumps. The larger pump, with a capacity of five tons, feeds hot or cold refrigerant through piping to an air handler, or fan coil unit. New ductwork in the basement penetrates the first floor structure to floor registers that serve the lower level of the house.

A second unit, with a capacity of 2.5 tons, sends its heated or cooled refrigerant to the third-floor attic by refrigerant lines running up through the former laundry chute. The air handler on the third floor feeds ductwork that penetrates vertically through the second-floor ceiling and horizontally through the third-floor walls to condition those spaces respectively. Each floor of the house is zoned separately for flexible control of the temperature. The ability to zone heating and cooling is one of the benefits of heat pump systems. Refrigerant can be run to separate fan coil units in each zone and controlled individually. This results in more precise control and greater comfort.

A by-product of geothermal heat pumps is waste heat. To take advantage of that heat, the inbound domestic cold water pipe from the water main was run through a tank of "waste heat" water from the heat pump system to preheat the incoming water before it gets to the hot water heater. This waste heat reduces the energy required to heat domestic hot water.

At the time of the interview with the architect, the geothermal system had gone through two summers and one winter season. Preliminary analysis shows that the heating and cooling of this 3,905-square-foot, three-story house cost about the same as the owner's previous 1,200-square-foot house. During very cold periods, the thermostat is programmed to switch over to the existing gas-fired boiler to supply hot water to the existing radiator system that was left in place. The radiators operate for a day or so until the exterior temperature rises to forty degrees or more to where the geothermal system can keep up again. The old radiators and gas-fired boiler were retained and used in lieu of adding electrical resistance heating that geothermal systems typically use in extreme cold weather. In St. Louis, the gas-fired boiler is cheaper than electric resistance heating. In extreme summer heat, when temperatures are frequently ninety to one hundred degrees with 90 percent humidity, it was difficult to hold the first floor below seventy-eight degrees. This is expected to improve when the eighty-year-old, single-pane windows are replaced with double-pane, low-E windows.

While this project was successful in the sense that it saved the owner considerable energy costs for heating and cooling, each GTHP case must be studied carefully. The payback on this system will be quite long, especially without tax credits and power company rebates. Unfortunately, this project just missed out on those 2009 tax credits. One must take into account the suitability of geothermal heat pumps for the design of the house, whether the house is existing or yet to be built, the area available for the wells, local soil conditions, and the availability of tax credits and gas company rebates. In other words, results will vary. The best advice is to hire a professional to assist in the design and construction of your geothermal heat pump system.

CHAPTER 10: HYDROELECTRIC ENERGY

Hydroelectric Dam

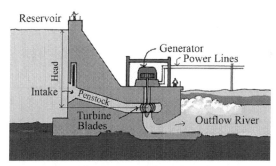

Cross Section—How It Works

Hydroelectric power generation is the first kind of renewable electricity generation ever used on a large scale. Hydroelectric power in the United States began in the 1800s on the Niagara River between Canada and the United States. The two neighbors have shared the water power and protected the scenic beauty of the falls since that time. At one time, Niagara was the largest power producer in the world, and it is still the largest hydro producer in New York State. Only a small percentage of the electric energy consumed is now generated by all combined U.S. hydroelectric dams, such as the one at Niagara. There are numerous dams along the Colorado River Basin that produce hydroelectricity, including the well-known Hoover and Glen Canyon dams. The Columbia and Snake River regions are also major hydroelectric power producers.

The picturesque old mills of the past, built alongside rivers, are an example of hydropower. Instead of generating electricity, the water wheel directly moved gears that turned the grinding wheel inside the mill to grind wheat into flour or corn into meal. Any location alongside a flowing stream could be converted to electric power generation for small communities or even a single-family home, although home use of hydro is rare.

This type of hydro generation is viable for direct individual home electricity production only for those fortunate folks who have a flowing stream passing through their property that could be impounded. As noted above, the amount of power that can be generated depends on the height through which the water can fall to the generator and on the volume and force of the water that can be redirected through the turbine. The water volume and the height of the reservoir needs to be considerable in order to make the construction of hydroelectric feasible and worth the expense.

Advantages

Most hydroelectric generating plants are very large and can supply vast amounts of electricity to thousands of people. They are largely nonpolluting and are inexhaustible, unless the creek runs dry. For most large hydroelectric dams on major rivers, this is usually not a problem, although in recent years severe and prolonged drought has caused the levels of lakes Mead and Powell on the Colorado River to drop as much as one hundred feet. The city of Las Vegas, at this time, is in the process of installing an intake for the city's water supply well below the existing intake because of the falling level of Lake Mead. Unless the water level stabilizes or recovers, Lake Mead may no longer supply the city's water. It is not known how the new intake will affect the power production of the dam.

Disadvantages

There are some disadvantages to hydroelectric power generation, in spite of the very positive advantages of being clean, nonpolluting, and constant. First, it is limited to areas where technology can take advantage of a source of flowing or impounded water. Water diversion and impoundment can cause environmental problems because of flooding. Flooded areas in the reservoir can be emitters of methane because of rotting vegetation. Changes in river flows can cause species of plants and fish to be threatened with extinction, especially those fish that spawn in the upper regions of the river. Fish can be killed going through the blades of the turbine. Lakes and other impounded bodies of water also take land from their original use. In China where more hydroelectric dams have been built than anywhere else in the world, many people have been forced from their homes and villages. As a country with a totalitarian government, China has no problem with opposition to new dams. In democratic countries, opposition can stop or delay hydroelectric projects.

Finally, building a hydroelectric dam is tremendously long and expensive project. In the United States, long drawn-out environmental studies are required, and relocating people can be difficult. Hydroelectric is not a short-term solution to alternative energies

Tidal Wave Generated Electrical Energy

Wave-generated energy is another example of hydroelectric power generation. It is broken down into two categories. The first category takes advantage of the ebb and flow of the tides twice daily. Generators with propellers, similar to wind turbines, are installed below the surface of the coastal waters. The generators can swing with the current as the tide comes in and flows out, generating electricity in any direction. On the coast of Florida, with its powerful Gulf Stream currents, wave generators could work very well.

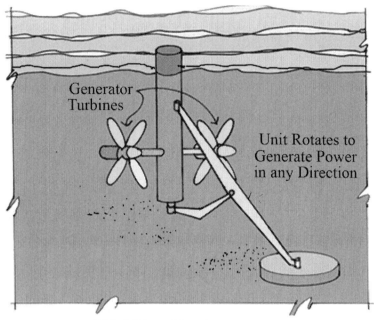

Tidal Wave Electic Generator

Where tides are not as strong, a narrow inlet can be dammed to impound the water at high tide and concentrate the flow. Wave generation could be used along our coastlines where large populations typically live, reducing the length of transmission lines. This technology is in its infancy but is being used in other parts of the world. One advantage of tidal energy generation over wind energy generation is that turbines are not visually prominent on the seascape.

Planning and public opinion buy-in is required. Tidal wave energy can interfere with accustomed access to open water for people and boats if an inlet is dammed for this purpose. The damming could also interfere with fish populations that use shallow inlets for spawning. The advantage to be weighed against these disadvantages is an inexhaustible source of free energy, once the initial cost is offset.

Wind-Driven Waves

The second form of wave-generated energy is dependent upon wind-driven waves that roll in to the shore and back out irrespective of the tides. One type involves generators that are anchored on the bottom and a long lever arm that moves back and forth with the waves drive a generator. Another type uses plungers to drive a generator, mounted on floats that rise and fall with the waves. Waves are nonpolluting, but waves dependent upon the wind are less reliable than tidal flows. They could still produce part of our electrical energy. Costal regions could benefit from these two alternatives.

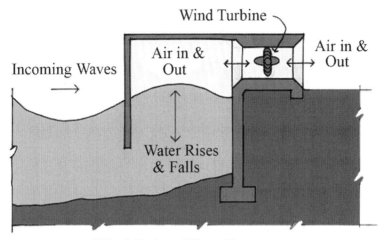

Wind-Driven Wave Generator

Yet another type of wind-driven wave generation is shore based. Incoming waves are captured in a chamber where the waves rise and fall, causing an airflow that turns a wind turbine that operates in either direction as the waves rise and fall.

Wave generation is a technology used in other countries but not to any great extent in the United States. Several designs take advantage of wave energy. Portugal has installed a system using a unique new technology along its coastline. The generator consists of a system of linked floats, like a chain of sausages. The connection between the floats contains the levers that turn the multiple generator turbines. Results are yet to be announced. It is certainly not something that the individual homeowner can take advantage of. It would require federal and or state participation to deploy, because of the cost of the technology and the location in our coastal waters, which could affect shipping and the environment. Their advantage is that there are no propellers involved in this type of generator so they are inherently safe. With our many miles of shoreline, this technology could produce a portion of our electrical energy requirements. After construction costs, the energy is free.

CHAPTER 11: BIOMASS ENERGY

Biomass refers to biological material, living or recently dead, that can be used as fuel directly, or turned into fuel through industrial processing. It excludes organic material that has been transformed by geological processes into coal or petroleum. Biomass materials include plants of all kinds, such as switch grass, hemp, corn, poplar, willow, sugarcane, oil palm, and even lowly algae.

Some of these alternative fuels, like ethanol or biodiesel that are made from biomass materials, have much less energy density than gasoline or fossil diesel fuels. For this reason, these fuels cannot support heavy trucks for over-the-road transportation of manufactured goods or farm produce, nor can they be used for mining or industrial purposes.

Anaerobic digestion, decaying in an oxygen-free atmosphere, can be used to produce methane gas from decaying biomass. Hydrogenation can also convert biomass to oil by using carbon monoxide (CO) and steam.

Corn, as well as other materials, such as sugar cane or wood wastes, can be used to produce methyl alcohol. This can also be used to make biodiesel fuel and ethanol. Corn ethanol production has to be subsidized because the cost of producing is about $8 per gallon. If all of our corn production were put to use to make ethanol, it would only replace 15 percent of our oil use. Using corn for fuel directly impacts food production. Currently the public eats a lot of corn, and corn sweeteners are used in many processed foods.

The argument that using biomass to produce ethanol necessarily impacts the cost of food is disputed. Experimentation with nonfood biomass is underway with such material as algae, which would not take fertile land out of food production. The unfortunate common denominator of most of the fuels made from biomass is that they consume a lot of energy in production. They also produce some noxious by-products when burned in internal combustion engines.

A chemical breakthrough, announced July 18, 2008, by Newscientist. com news service, is said to make it possible to convert waste products, such as saw dust, into liquid hydrocarbons like ethanol and biodiesel. Producing ethanol from cellulose, such as saw dust, could relieve the pressure on food crop production. This is good news as long as waste products are used, and trees are not cut down specifically for fuel production. The bad news is that these fuels still pollute.

Biofuel is a growing industry in Malaysia; the forests are being laid waste in order to use the land to grow oil palms to produce biodiesel. The sad truth is that the biofuel that is produced from the palm oil is resulting in a net loss of CO_2 absorption, compared to the original forests.

Deforestation or urbanization destroys part of the biomass and removes it from the natural cycle. When destroyed and not renewed through new growth, vegetation cannot absorb the carbon dioxide and release oxygen. If you burn wood (biomass) in your furnace or wood stove, it releases approximately the same amount of carbon dioxide that it would if it decayed (biodegradation) on the forest floor, except that it does so more quickly and sends smoke pollution (particulate matter) into the atmosphere. Some urban centers have bans on burning wood in fireplaces because the smoke can be an irritant to people with respiratory problems. Wood is not necessarily a cheap fuel, depending on where you live. If you are a farmer, living in a wooded area, you could conceivably burn wood for heating and cooking, sustaining your needs for a long time through regrowth. City dwellers do not have this option.

There are stoves and furnaces that burn wood pellets, which are made from manufacturing waste from furniture manufacturing and logging. These pellets burn slightly more cleanly than cord wood, producing 1.2 grams of particulate per hour, which is well below the EPA wood burning limit of 7.5 grams.

Fossil fuels are not part of the natural cycle, because they have been out of the atmosphere for a very long time. When burned, they add to the atmosphere's carbon load.

Biomass fuels could become viable alternatives if those fuels could meet the following criteria: (1) they must overcome the high cost of production, (2) overcome the impact on food production, (3) use no fossil fuels for manufacture, (4) eliminate polluting emissions when burned, and (5) overcome their low-energy density. They could then become viable alternative fuels. That seems like too many ifs to be realistic. Polluting fuels need to be phased out altogether, if possible. They do have value as interim solutions to bridge the gap from fossil fuels to clean energy sources for small personal vehicles.

On July 27, 2009, an article by Kevin Bullis in MIT's Technology Review, announced startling developments in the field of biomass energy production. A new start-up company based in Cambridge, MA, named Joule Biotechnologies, claims they can make 20,000 gallons of biofuels per year per acre from genetically altered micro-organisms. This is phenomenal since so far only algae-based biofuels come even close to this efficiency, producing from 2,000 to 6,000 gallons per acre per year. This new process is of the scale of production that can make biofuels a viable substitute for fossil fuels. Can biofuels produced in this way replace all fossil fuels for transportation when production is scaled up? Only time will tell. No mention was made of the bio-fuel's energy density or whether it would be enough to power over the road trucks.

The process involves growing genetically engineered micro-organisms in specially designed photo-bio reactors. They use energy from the sun to convert carbon dioxide and water *directly* into ethanol or bio diesel. The organisms excrete the fuel, which can then be collected using conventional chemical-separation technologies. Amazingly it doesn't have to be refined. Note the fact that it uses carbon dioxide in the process? The microbes are fed concentrated carbon dioxide--which can come from a power plant, for example. This is exciting news. *The process makes fuel and absorbs CO2.* It was not explained whether the burning of this product, the production of which used carbon dioxide, would release more CO2.

The best current algae fuel technologies to be competitive with fossil fuels would have to cost over $800 a barrel. Joule claims that its process will be competitive with crude oil at $50 a barrel which is very close to the present cost of oil. Algae has to be collected and processed in a batch while Joule's micro-organisms produce fuel non-stop without collecting and processing them. It is interesting to note that Exxon Mobil is interested in this technology. Exxon represents the scale of company that could produce quantities sufficient to free us from fossil fuels, or make a serious dent in them. The company expects to produce ethanol on a commercial scale by the end of 2010. Large-scale demonstration of hydrocarbon-fuels production would follow in 2011. The only barrier to starting a large scale plant is securing funding.

CHAPTER 12: HYDROGEN

Hydrogen is the most abundant material in the universe. Seventy-five percent of all of the universe's elemental mass is hydrogen. It is the material of which most stars are made. It is in water and occurs in most organic compounds, chemicals, and particularly acids. There has been a lot of talk about using hydrogen as an alternative to fossil fuels. Hydrogen can be burned directly in internal combustion engines or as the fuel for fuel cells. It is abundant, has a high-energy density, burns CO_2 free, and can be made from a number of materials. It burns so cleanly that the only by-product of burning it is water and heat, and the flame is so clean it is invisible. If a leak in a hydrogen system catches fire, it requires a flame detector to tell where it is. It sounds like the ideal alternative fuel. So what is the catch?

As attractive as it seems as a fuel, hydrogen it is not an energy source. It has to be extracted from some other material and right now commercial bulk hydrogen is usually produced by the steam reforming of natural gas or methane. The process involves steam reacting with methane at high temperatures to yield carbon monoxide (CO), a deadly gas, and hydrogen (H_2). The high-temperature steam needed for the process has to come from somewhere, which means another energy source is required. It could be solar heat, which would help make the process cheaper, except for the expense of building and maintaining the solar collecting plant. Hydrogen is widely used to make anhydrous ammonia fertilizer for the farming industry. Because of the hydrogen that ammonia possesses, it could also be used as fuel for fuel cells, given a means to extract it.

It makes little sense to take natural gas, already a usable fuel although somewhat polluting, and process it more to turn it into hydrogen to burn in internal combustion engines. This merely adds a process and additional cost. Methane is already a fuel that is much easier to handle with known technology.

The production of hydrogen by electrolysis is very simple, but unfortunately the resulting hydrogen has less energy content than is required to produce it. It involves placing a metal electrode in an acid. The hydrogen bubbles up out of the acid, but the metal electrode is used up and has to be replaced periodically.

The cost of producing hydrogen is just the beginning of the negatives for its use as a fuel. The infrastructure costs associated with a full conversion to a hydrogen economy would be substantial. Hydrogen, because of its interaction with metals and other compounds, tends to cause some metals used in pipelines to become brittle and leak, or worse. Gas tanks for liquid hydrogen would need to be three times the size of normal gas tanks because of hydrogen's low molecular density. Hydrogen contains less energy than gasoline or diesel on a per-volume basis, in spite of its high energy density, so it is difficult to store enough hydrogen safely onboard a vehicle to travel more than two hundred miles. Other challenges include customer acceptance of hydrogen and the infrastructure required to transport and store it. Many technical questions need to be resolved before hydrogen can become a universal energy for transportation.

CHAPTER 13: FUEL CELLS

Fuel cells are not really an alternative fuel. They are a means for producing electricity to do the work. Fuel cells combine hydrogen and oxygen to produce electricity through an electrochemical reaction. The hydrogen does not burn but combines with oxygen to generate electricity. The technology is not new either. The first one was built in 1839 by an amateur scientist.

More recently, the U.S. space program has used them to power the Gemini and Apollo space crafts. No CO_2 or other pollutants are produced when a fuel cell runs on hydrogen. The only exhaust is water and heat. In principle, a fuel cell operates like a battery. Unlike a battery, a fuel cell does not store energy. It will produce energy in the form of electricity and heat as long as fuel is supplied.

How a fuel cell works: The technology is a little difficult to understand, but here it is if you are interested. A fuel cell consists of two electrodes, called the anode on one side and the cathode on the other, with an electrolyte between them. Oxygen passes over one electrode and hydrogen over the other, generating electricity while exhausting only water and heat.

A fuel cell system includes a fuel reformer, a device that can transform hydrogen-rich fuels from any hydrocarbon fuel, such as natural gas, methanol, and even gasoline. If they are run on fossil fuels, the cells can then produce some pollution.

Since the fuel cell relies on chemistry and not combustion, emissions from this type of a system would still be much smaller than emissions from the cleanest fuel combustion processes. See Fuel Cells 2000 at www.fuelcells.org for further information.

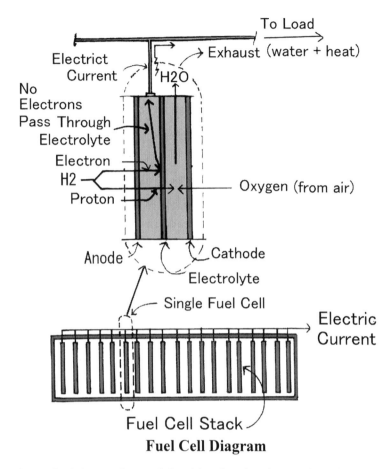

Fuel Cell Diagram

Since fuel is not burned in this simple electrochemical process, a fuel cell can operate quietly, virtually pollution and maintenance free. While a typical automobile engine captures 15–20 percent of gasoline's chemical energy, a fuel cell can convert 45–60 percent of its fuel's energy into usable power.

There are some problems with using fuels cells for automobiles at this time. Major drawbacks include the cost of manufacturing them, the cost of producing the hydrogen, and the distance that the automobile can go on a single tank when there are virtually no refueling stations at this time. Because hydrogen has a low density, it has to be compressed into large fuel tanks, and this limits the amount an automobile can carry.

Scientists believe that cost-effective fuel cells may be available within five years. The goal of scientists is to learn to mass produce them to bring the costs down because they are prohibitive at this time. Refueling stations will also be critical to using hydrogen for cars.

Fuel Cells in Buildings

Fuel cells make sense in stationary applications like buildings for a variety of reasons. Large storage tanks present less of a problem for stationary installations, and fuel delivery could be by pipeline directly to the point of use. They deliver unparalleled fuel efficiencies, where the waste thermal energy is harvested for heating and air conditioning purposes. In addition to clean, quiet operation, fuel cells offer highly reliable, high-quality electricity. If a blackout occurs, they will keep essential mechanical components operating.

Matsushita Electric Industrial Company, parent company of the Panasonic brand, claims it plans to sell two hundred thousand fuel cell units for domestic use by 2015. The cost of a residential fuel cell power plant is about $3,000 per kilowatt. In addition, the hydrogen fuel to power the fuel cell would have to be supplied. If used in connection with a photovoltaic system to store energy for nighttime and cloudy days, the system could be very effective as an alternative to being connected to the grid with a battery backup system.

Most fuel cell research has been focused on generating electricity for electric cars. If the technology could produce fuel cells that were cheaper, they could become feasible for homes. Right now they are one of the most expensive of all current alternative fuel generators. They hold promise as production increases and more applications use them, bringing the cost down.

A recent breakthrough has produced a methanol fuel cell so small that it can be used for cell phones and other small handheld appliances. Testing has taken it to 2700 hours with a power degradation of less than 15 percent. The cell uses liquid methanol and is very safe. They have been approved for airline travel. Initially scheduled for industrial uses, the cells' long lives make them seem ideal for military and GPS devices. They are called Mobion fuel cells and are produced by MTI Micro who is partnering with NeoSolar to produce consumer prototypes.

Research in the field of fuel cells has recently yielded new designs that can use other fuels, including biomass.

CHAPTER 14: NUCLEAR ENERGY

The Arguments for Nuclear Energy

It has been twelve years since a new nuclear power plant has come on line in the United States. The recent high cost of fossil fuels has prompted renewed interest in nuclear power generation. Nuclear energy is a clean, nonpolluting way to generate electricity. It releases no CO_2 or other green house gases. The technology is well proven, having been around since the 1950s. It is constant, and theoretically, we have enough fissile material to last for thousands of years. If we can't produce what we need, we can buy uranium from friendly countries, like Canada and Australia.

Nuclear power has the advantages of providing a secure major source of energy that does not emit air pollution, including CO_2, while generating electricity. Nuclear is more reliable and constant than wind or solar energy and doesn't require storage of power like those alternatives do. The cost of producing electricity from nuclear material is often quoted as less than coal.

The Arguments against Nuclear Energy

Nuclear plants are expensive to build, with capital costs just below that of coal plants. If a carbon tax is implemented, nuclear power becomes competitive with coal-generated electricity.

The problem is that those who quote cheap costs for nuclear seldom take into account the resulting pollution from mining operations, the cost of plant decommissioning, and storage of spent fuel. In order to obtain funding for new plants, proponents demand subsidies and loan guarantees from the government for 100 percent of the project debt.

Opponents are concerned that the expansion of nuclear plants would reduce the investment in renewable energy technologies. If the goal is to cover 80 percent of the world's present energy demands with nuclear plants, thousands of nuclear plants would be required at a price of several billion dollars each.

Another negative aspect of nuclear plants that use water for cooling is they can overheat during very hot weather. This can require shutting down the plant or reducing its production of electricity just when you need it most for airconditioning. If the hot water is released into a stream or lake, it can result in substantial fish kills and other ecological damage.

The primary pollution produced by nuclear energy comes from mining the uranium. According to the *San Francisco Chronicle*, in a recent article, the U.S. Department of Energy estimates that 500 billion gallons of ground water remains contaminated with uranium and other toxic chemicals in thirty-six states from the mining of uranium during the cold war to make bombs. Another 800 million gallons of waste from uranium mines and weapons plants lie buried in landfills, trenches, and unlined tanks. More than two billion cubic feet of contaminated sediment remain to be cleaned up. The sediment is a mountain of toxic dirt two thousand times larger than the Great Pyramid at Giza.

Currently scientists are frantically researching the use of human-friendly microorganisms that would digest soluble radioactive material to turn it into a solid that would not seep into ground water.

France, who produces 78 percent of its electricity by nuclear, has experienced incidents that released radioactive material into the air, resulting in plants being shut down from time to time. It is not known what effect the leaks have had on the local public, despite studies that have been implemented. Disastrous accidents have been few, most notably Chernobyl in Russia and Three Mile Island in the United States. These have made it difficult to convince the public that nuclear reactors are safe.

Nuclear plants have been enclosed in concrete containment buildings in this country and surrounded by high double fences, which are electronically monitored. This does not take into account a terrorist attack from the air. Plans for the threat "Design Basis" are secret, so it isn't known what kind of force plants are able to defend against. If waste from a plant were left unguarded, the material could be stolen and used for dirty bombs.

Breeder reactors are currently being discussed as an option, because a breeder reactor can utilize spent fuel from normal uranium reactors by adding plutonium to the uranium. After the initial fuel charge of plutonium, it requires only natural (or even depleted) uranium to keep it running. This results in the reaction creating more fuel than it uses. We could reuse the spent uranium waiting to be stored in a facility like Yucca Mountain and not have to rely on new uranium.

One serious problem with breeder reactors is that they can't use water as a coolant like regular reactors can. They use liquid metals instead. One coolant being used is liquid sodium, an extremely dangerous material that burns or explodes when it comes into contact with air or water. It therefore has to be sealed in a containment vessel. Other liquid metals used as coolants are mercury and lead. With liquid sodium, an accident could be disastrous. Mercury and lead are also both serious pollutants.

The breeder reactors are extremely expensive because of the safety precautions they require. The recycling of spent fuel from plants that use uranium was banned in the administration of Jimmy Carter due to concerns about terrorists stealing the plutonium that recycling creates. We built only one breeder reactor in the United States back in the 1950s, and it was run only for a short time.

The plutonium that results from reprocessing nuclear fuel is one of the most dangerous materials known to man, and is currently used to make nuclear weapons. The recycling of uranium from conventional reactors to create fuel for breeder reactors results in the largest source of radioactive emissions in the nuclear fuel chain, according to Mycle Schneider, French nuclear policy consultant. He maintains that it adds to the collective global dose of radiation in the atmosphere.

Uranium, the fuel normally used in conventional reactors, exists in finite quantities, and only 8 percent of what is used in the United States is produced here. Buying uranium from other countries would not reduce our outflow of assets. In other words, we would be trading a dependence on foreign oil for a dependence on foreign uranium. Nate Lewis, professor of chemistry at California Institute of Technology and editor in chief. of the Royal Society of Chemistry journal, *Energy and Environmental Science*, claims that to replace our reliance on coal, gas, and oil would require us to build a new nuclear plant every day for the next fifty years. With our production of uranium at only 8 percent of what we use, one wonders where we could possibly get the fuel to run that many plants, even if they could be built so quickly. We would need to perfect the operation of breeder reactors, using the spent fuel from the normal reactors, which could give us an almost unlimited supply of nuclear fuel.

The National Environment Agency claims that we have a sixty-thousand-year supply of uranium in the United States, citing resources of 5.5 million metric tons and 10.5 million tons that remain undiscovered. What a strange statement. If it is undiscovered, how can they tell how much is there to be discovered? There are disturbing questions here.

Disposal—A Serious Quandary

Whether or not breeder reactors prove to be feasible, there is still a serious problem with disposing of the waste. The only disposal site currently under development in the United States is at Yucca Mountain, Nevada, previously due to open in 2017. Controversy has delayed the deployment of this storage facility. After taking office, President Obama promised to shut down Yucca Mountain. Nuclear utilities are now storing spent fuel in huge concrete-encased casks on site at nuclear plants. Each cask contains ten tons of waste. A 1,000-megawatt reactor discharges enough spent fuel to fill two of these casks every year at a cost of $1 million apiece. The cost of "recycling" the waste that would be stored in Yucca Mountain is estimated to be between $50 and $100 billion. Transporting the waste to a facility halfway across the country for storage exposes millions of people to the risk of a nuclear spill or even terrorist attacks.

Recycling

In the 1980s, France began reprocessing spent nuclear fuel from Belgium, Germany, Japan, the Netherlands, and Switzerland, as well as for their own nuclear plants. Initially the reprocessed material was to be sent back to the countries from which it had come to be used in breeder reactors. Without operating breeder reactors in those countries, the recycled material remains a useless waste material that presents a serious storage problem. France now processes and stores only the spent French fuel. This reprocessed fuel is about 10 percent of the volume of that which comes from the plants using new uranium fuel, but the reprocessed material is more expensive to use than new uranium.

Besides the cost factor, the plutonium resulting from reprocessing spent fuel still has to be dealt with. Because reprocessing is expensive and reduces the waste products only marginally, the disposal problem still exists for much of the waste.

In the United States, new nuclear power plants receive subsidies, and the approval process has been streamlined. As the price of gasoline rises, the public view has become more forgiving of nuclear power as a source of energy, despite memories of Three Mile Island, the cost, disposal problems, and the inherent danger of plutonium falling into terrorists' hands.

In 2008, the administration was pushing for recycling of spent nuclear fuel for use in breeder reactors in an attempt to resolve the problem of our appetite for fossil fuels. Presently, there are no operational breeder reactors in the United States. Such facilities would have to be built.

Nuclear energy is a complicated alternative to coal or natural gas for electrical generation. It is not really cheap, and it cannot be expanded quickly. Like many of the other alternatives, opinions and compelling arguments abound on either side of the debate over nuclear energy. We need our best minds to examine all aspects of the subject, taking into account the cost-to-benefit ratio, safety, disposal of waste, and national security.

Oak Ridge National Laboratory (ORNL) is working on the development of a new process for recycling spent nuclear waste that can utilize recycled fuel in existing reactors. If successful, the process would reduce the amount of plutonium produced. Dana Christensen, associate laboratory director for energy and engineering sciences at ORNL, claims that "in the reactor we make some new plutonium, but if we design and run the reactor properly, we can eventually destroy more plutonium than we make."

Until such time as these recycling techniques are perfected, we should continue to pursue less costly and less polluting alternatives that create no waste products. ORNL should certainly continue their research because nuclear power will undoubtedly contribute to a fossil-fuel-free strategy for the future. Certainly there is already considerable nuclear waste that needs to be processed.

Cold Fusion—Fact or Fantasy?

Recently a type of nuclear energy called cold fusion has reappeared as an option to the intensively hot and dangerous process of generating electricity using uranium. Several years back a couple of physicists claimed to have created heat from cold fusion in a lab at room temperature. They were susequently discredited after no other scientists could duplicate the process.

Recently another scientist has claimed that he created heat from cold fusion. It has fostered a heated debate, but no real, verifiable, usable heat from the process. If cold fusion can be developed it would be the solution to all of our energy problems and require the input of very little fuel. Much skepticism exists in the scientific community. Some incredible breakthrough may eventually solve the development of cold fusion. Until that time it seems like a real long shot. It's a worthwhile target of experimentation, and I wish those scientists willing to devote their lives to trying for that breakthrough all the best of luck.

CHAPTER 15: THE FALLACY OF CLEAN COAL AND GAS

Clean coal is a term much used by those whose fortunes are tied up in coal, specifically coal producers. Coal is not now, nor will it ever be, clean. It is not considered an alternative energy source either. It can be made less polluting by removing some of the pollutants and capturing CO_2 at the smoke stack, but it will still be polluting. Carbon capture is essential with coal. If we must burn coal, all possible technologies should be considered to remove as many pollutants as possible. The use of coal to generate electricity uses the world's most polluting fuel. It cannot, by any stretch of the imagination, be considered a viable alternative by the criteria set up in Chapter 3. The only good news about coal is that we have an abundant supply of it, greater than most other countries. It can be made *cleaner* by chemically washing impurities from it and capturing carbon dioxide and other pollutants at the smoke stack. After all of this is done, it will still pollute, just not quite as much.

It isn't clear, as with most energy sources, just how much we have left in terms of our coal reserves. In 1970 we were told that there was a 250-year supply. In 2008, estimates of our coal reserves were pegged at one hundred years. Coal seems to have been used up to the tune of 60 percent in under forty years. That would seem to tell us that we may have less than a hundred years' supply left. These figures don't say if they account for projections of the growth of population and for proposed new uses of coal to replace oil.

Coal is a relatively cheap fuel. The disadvantages of burning coal in industry and for generation of electricity are its pollution of the atmosphere, the cost of making it less polluting, and the need for CO_2 capture and storage. These disadvantages are coupled with the pollution of the land and ground water by the mining process used in the production of coal. Together, these problems are a great incentive for finding other fuels to replace coal.

On December 22, 2008, the Kingston Tennessee Fossil Plant, a coal-fired electricity-generating plant of the Tennessee Valley Authority, spilled more than a billion gallons of toxic sludge from an earthen dam. The spill covered some three hundred acres of land as it made its way to the Emory River.

Toxic sludge is created by a smokestack-scrubbing process that captures ash that used to go up in smoke. On its path, the spill destroyed and/or damaged at least forty-five homes and other properties. There are many similar facilities around the country, most of which claim to be following federal regulations for storage of coal ash. Many environmental advocates say that the regulations are inadequate, or even a joke.

The Kingston disaster is said to be bigger in its impact than the Exxon Valdez oil spill in Alaska. The U.S. Energy Department statistics reveal that 156 coal-fired power plants store ash in hundreds of surface ponds over thirty-two states. Some of this waste, called fly ash, is being incorporated into the manufacture of cement. Increasingly, coal ash is being sold for construction fill, mine reclamation, and farm uses, such as improving a soil's ability to hold water. The bulk of it goes into ponds because it is a cheap solution for dealing with this by-product of burning coal that used to go into the atmosphere. Now instead of polluting the air, the Kingston ash pollutes the area's water.

Natural Gas

Because biofuels have too low an energy density for over-the-road trucks and other heavy equipment, we need to find a fuel for this type of transportation that has the required energy density. Right now, that fuel appears to be nonrenewable natural gas.

Compressed Natural Gas (CNG)

T. Boone Pickens, the Texas oil man, recently converted to a proponent of wind energy and advocated the use of compressed natural gas (CNG) for transportation, because he feels that biofuels do not have the energy density to power large over-the-road transport trucks. This is one of the pillars of the Pickens plan.

We have fairly substantial supplies of natural gas. It is the fuel that heats our homes and is often encountered when drilling oil wells. In some cases, natural gas was simply burned off to get rid of it in the oil recovery process. That was very wasteful, since it could be captured and piped to cities where it is a valuable fuel to heat our buildings and homes.

Natural gas or methane can be used to power cars and trucks with a simple conversion from gasoline to compressed gas (CNG). Fueling stations can easily be set up, even in homes that already have natural gas piped to them. It is a cleaner burning fuel than coal or diesel, and engines burning it require much less maintenance as a result. It has a high energy density making it a choice for heavy trucks. Compressing it makes it much more suitable for trucks. It is usually compressed to two hundred times atmospheric pressure at room temperature, which keeps the size of tanks reasonable and allows a good range on a tank of fuel. The current disadvantages are that more fueling stations will be required and some pollution is emitted when it is burned, but less than gasoline. Natural gas is also a finite resource and will someday be depleted. Methane is generated in many processes and would continue to be available upon capture.

Coal to Liquid Fuel (CTL)

Fuels to power heavy equipment can also be produced from coal, called coal to liquid (CTL), which can be substituted for gasoline or diesel. The process turns coal into a liquid fuel by combining coal under pressure with steam and oxygen, and then introducing catalysts, processing it into gasoline or diesel fuel. This results in a cleaner burning fuel than diesel or gasoline, but not pollution or CO_2 free. These fuels are also more biodegradable. The infrastructure required to handle them is the same as gasoline and diesel, so no new systems for distribution are needed. The cost of CTL fuels is competitive with oil with oil at $35 per barrel. If crude oil climbs to $75 or more, CTL will be decidedly a cheaper choice.

Liquid Natural Gas (LNG)

Liquefied natural gas is another product made from natural gas. It has the same lower emission advantages as natural gas but is made in a slightly different way. The natural gas is turned into a liquid by cooling it to a very low temperature, –260 degrees Fahrenheit, or –163 degrees Celsius. The process compresses the gas to 1/600th of the volume of the natural gas that comes from regular distribution pipes for home use. This reduction in volume makes it less bulky and easier to transport in tanker trucks or rail cars. LNG has a high energy density, which lends its use to heavy trucks. There is also less variation in quality in LNG than in CNG. One disadvantage of LNG is that it is heavier and bulkier to store than gasoline. Storage facilities must be insulated to keep it from boiling off and evaporating, resulting in higher cost. It will also boil off in vehicles that sit unused for several days. It is best used in vehicles kept in more or less constant use.

Liquefied Petroleum Gas (LPG)

Under half of the LPG used in the United States comes from the petroleum refining industry as a by-product. The rest comes from natural gas processing. Most, 90 percent, is produced here in the U.S., and the rest comes from Canada. It is bottled and stored at twenty times atmospheric pressure. It is often called propane and is used in cars and trucks, barbeque grills, and for cooking in homes not connected to natural gas pipelines.

LPG advantages are that it is widely available, cleaner burning in vehicles reducing pollution and maintenance, contains a fairly high energy density, and is largely domestically supplied. Disadvantages are that it has a lower energy density than gasoline requiring a larger fuel tank. Because its source is partly petroleum, it is polluting. It costs more for vehicles to run on LPG.

Coal-Eating Bugs to Gas

The Massachusetts Institute of Technology's *Technology Review* published an article on January 8, 2009, reporting that a Golden, Colorado, company and another in San Antonio, Texas, were developing a process whereby microorganisms were being used to convert coal to methane (natural gas). Burning the converted gas cuts CO_2 emissions to half that of coal.

CHAPTER 16: COMBINED HEAT AND POWER

Combined heat and power, or cogeneration systems are not really alternative fuel sources. They are something of a mixed bag. They can become an alternative means of generating electricity if a building is not located where it can connect to the power grid. They can also be used as a power source for a facility like a hospital that can't afford to lose power. Most such buildings have emergency generators that do the same job, but CHP systems furnish the power all of the time. Prior to this time of diminishing supplies of fossil fuels, they were used mostly in very large buildings that wanted self-sufficiency in terms of electric power. Now they are being considered for smaller installations and even homes.

Combined heat and power systems are basically generators that use internal combustion engines, burning some type of hydrocarbon fuel, to produce electricity. The waste heat can also be used to heat water for domestic water systems or even space heating. The main problem in this day and age is with the fuel used to run the generator. Natural gas is an obvious choice because of the ease of delivery, but other fuels can be used, such as diesel or gasoline. These are all polluting to some degree. If they ran on less polluting or nonpolluting fuels, then they could be considered a type of alternative source of electrical power.

Sea World marine park in San Diego, California, operates a cogeneration plant. It provides them a reliable source of electric power to ensure all of the pumps are operating to keep the animal habitats functioning. If Sea World lost power for a lengthy period of time, its animals, collected and/or grown at great expensive, would be at risk. Down time for the park could also result in major loss of ticket revenue, which in turn would affect its ability to care for the animals.

The advantages of a CHP system would be that a building can be completely off the grid. They rely on a cheap fuel to be feasible, but on the plus side, could avoid any and all power outages. The main drawback to these systems is the cost of the equipment and their use of fuels that emit pollutants. The systems also require regular maintenance. A cheap, nonpolluting fuel could make them feasible for such installations.

CHAPTER 17: NEW TECHNOLOGY

Not every alternative energy source is viable in every location. Many are not applicable to homeowners because of the installation, equipment, maintenance costs, and the difficulty of retrofitting an existing home. If you are building a new home, you have more opportunities for cost-effective, energy-efficient design. Conservation and alternative energy can and should be built in. Those of us who already own older homes have fewer opportunities and greater challenges, but we can still take some measures to save energy and money.

If you live in an apartment and your power is metered separately, requiring you to pay your own utility bills, you definitely will want to conserve energy. Yes, apartment dwellers need to save energy too. If you are looking for a new apartment, there are things for you to consider.

If you are building new or just updating, take the time to do some research first. It will pay you in the long run for your time and effort. There are many new, innovative ideas for energy-saving materials and equipment. The World Wide Web is the best place to start, because it often takes a while for the market place to get the message about new products. Talk to the employees at your local building supply store too. They can be a good source of information. A few ideas are listed here, and there are very likely more to be found. Do not forget that siting your new building is very important for either conservation or alternatives.

Staggered-Stud Wall Construction

This construction technique, used primarily in very cold climates because of additional cost, employs double-stud walls where the two separate rows of studs support the inside and outside wall surfaces independently with no direct structural connection between them, except at the top and bottom. A continuous six-inch insulating blanket fills the void, providing a very well-insulated exterior wall. Extra material and labor are required, but the energy-saving benefits make it well worth the extra cost over the life of the building. In normal single-stud wall construction, cold is transferred directly through the wall at every stud by conduction. This type of wall should also employ double- or triple-glazed windows and thermal break frames and sash. Energy savings can be significant in any season.

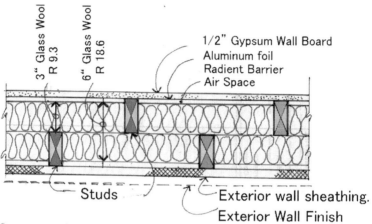

Staggerd Stud Wall Construction

Staggered-Stud Wall

It is not necessarily new technology, but it is innovative in the way that the inside and outside wall surfaces are separated, reducing heat/cold transefer between the two.

A recent innovation for normal single-stud wall construction places an adhesive backed thin, insulating strip over the inside of each stud wall before dry wall is applied. The strips cost about $1 per lineal foot. The material, called Thermablock, increases the thermal insulation of the wall by 30 percent. See www.thermalblock.com.

Innovative Products

Some good products have been on the market for years but were never marketed in the United States. One such product is autoclaved, aerated concrete block, used to build homes in Scandinavia for decades. Autoclaving is a fancy name for cooking in a pressure cooker. The process, which includes mixing aluminum powder with the cement, creates a concrete block full of tiny hydrogen bubbles. It provides thermal and acoustic insulation, and is fire and termite resistant. The hydrogen is trapped in the concrete, so there is no danger of fire or explosion.

There are several products under the category of insulating concrete forms (ICF) available for building that provide inside and outside insulation, as well as the form for pouring concrete walls, all as part of the integrated product. They all have one thing in common in that they produce a reinforced concrete wall with excellent insulating properties that is very efficient for noise reduction, strength, and thermal resistance. The outside can be finished with stucco, masonry, or any other exterior material. The inside can be finished with plaster, drywall, or paneling. A product called Mikey Block has the best insulating properties of these systems because the design has the least concrete connecting between the inside and outside wall surfaces.

Mikey Blocks – Insulating Concrete Forms

For frame construction, there is a product, made by Superior Wood Systems, that replaces some of the traditional solid wood structural framing members. Headers over exterior openings are made with foam insulation sandwiched between two wood members. It helps to prevent transmission of heat or cold directly through the wall framing.

Exterior insulation and finish systems (EIFS), also called synthetic stucco, is an exterior wall finish system that places rigid foam insulation on the outside of the wall, which is the best possible place for it to be. It can be applied to wood frame construction as well as metal studs or masonry. This is not a do-it-yourself project, as very careful flashing and sealing needs to be done by expert installers to prevent serious, even catastrophic, future damage due to possible leaks and water infiltration, especially with wood frame construction.

Another product that places the insulation on the outside of the wall is a custom-contoured underlayment designed to fit snugly behind many brands of vinyl siding. The product can also be obtained with the vinyl siding securely attached to the insulation. There are several manufacturers of similar products. They can improve the thermal resistance (R value) of the wall from R2.8 to 4.5.

There is a paint additive, developed for the space program, which can turn paint into a thermal barrier. It consists of miniscule ceramic spheres that are hollow and contain a vacuum. They are so tiny that a quantity of them resembles wheat flour. Mixed into any paint, they become an effective thermal barrier. This is due in part to the sphere's vacuum and in part to the manner in which the tiny spheres compact together to form a reflective barrier. Ordinary paint has voids in it when dry. The spheres reportedly fill all voids blocking the transmission of heat through the paint. The material can be used inside on walls and ceilings or outside on side walls or roof surfaces. Look for Hy Tech Thermacell Insulating paint additive. A word of caution is in order. Check it out on a small inconspicuous location before committing to any large exposed areas. There are mixed opinions about this product, and it would be wise to seek out people on the Internet who have used the product to get an opinion based on actual use.

These are a few new products, some of which could help reduce energy use. For centuries most buildings have been built the same way, either with masonry of some sort or with lumber. While stick-built lumber buildings and homes are cheaper than masonry, easier to insulate, and quicker to build, technology in the age of space exploration should be able to devise better methods. Even so, some ancient ways to build may still be relevant to our modern world.

CHAPTER 18: OLD TECHNOLOGY

Building with Dirt—Rammed Earth

Some old technologies warrant being revisited. New is not always better. Houses constructed of rammed earth have been built for centuries. Rammed earth construction refers to the use of material from the site, namely dirt or clay, which is placed between wall forms and then compacted mechanically or by hand to form a hard, dense wall. Some type of binder, such as cement, is often used if soil types are not adequate. The advantage of rammed earth construction is that the material is largely free, it does not have to be trucked in, and no energy is consumed in its manufacture. It can be covered with stucco or left exposed to the atmosphere in dry climates. Insulation can be added in several ways, either inside the building, between the walls, or on the outside with an exterior insulation and facing system (EIFS). The walls are usually quite thick, creating a natural heat sink that evens out the wide temperature swings in walls.

Adobe Bricks

Adobe is a similar product that has also been used for centuries, and made from local materials. Mud is mixed with straw or horsehair as a binder. The material is then formed into blocks or bricks, and dried in the sun. Adobe is still used as a building material in dry climates. Indigenous people and early settlers have long used it in the American Southwest. Part of the Great Wall of China is made from adobe where masonry was not available. Adobe also consumes no fuel in its production, and it emits no pollution.

Straw Bale Construction

When you think of a straw house, you probably think of the three little pigs. The straw houses discussed here are not going to be blown down easily. They are sturdy and can be designed in most any style, although they lend themselves best to the Southwest style stucco look. They are very popular in New Zealand, but over six hundred straw homes are located in the United States.

Construction is very simple. There are two basic types. One involves a post and beam structural system, and the bales of straw are simply filled in between the posts and beams. A concrete footing is constructed on top of which the bales of straw are stacked to the desired height. In the second type, the hay bales form the structural wall. Roof framing is placed directly on top of the bales on a wood header. The straw must be kept dry during construction and then sealed with stucco inside and out. These walls end up about two feet thick. The insulating value of the straw bales is R40 to R55, or about three times that of a normal wall, partly due to the nature of the material, which contains voids, and partly because of the thickness of the walls. Heating and cooling costs are very favorable as is the cost of wall materials.

A Web site at http://www.strawhomes.com has more information including a list of frequently asked questions about straw homes. Another site can provide additional information at http://www.strawbale.com.

Straw homes can even be two stories high, but if you plan to build it yourself, designing it for a single-story makes construction much easier. The types of straw commonly used are oat, wheat, and barley. In addition to stucco, other materials such as stone or brick can be used as finished wall surfaces as long as the straw bales are sealed from the weather.

Before committing a lot of time and money to a project with these unconventional materials, thoroughly research your local building codes.

CHAPTER 19: EFFICIENCY AND CONSERVATION

Manufactured Savings

Every little reduction in energy usage adds up more than you might think. The American Council for an Energy-Efficient Economy (ACEEE) recently produced a report which speculates that energy-efficient technologies can effectively reduce our energy consumption by 25 to 30 percent in the next twenty to twenty-five years. The report stated that efficient technology will have already slashed our energy consumption by half from 1970 levels by the end of 2008. What did we do to achieve this amazing result? We forced the auto industry, kicking and screaming every step of the way, to make automobiles more efficient, getting better gas mileage. We also developed new efficiency standards for air conditioners, furnaces, water heaters, and kitchen appliances, and developed new energy-efficient lighting fixtures. Can we do more? Absolutely, and we must.

In a recent announcement on November 13, 2008, MIT's *Technology Review* announced that a Vancouver, BC, startup company, ExRo, had developed a new kind of generator for wind turbines that increases the output of wind turbines by 50 percent. *Technology Review* also recently reported a new wind turbine design based on a jet engine that could reduce the cost of wind turbines and increase their efficiency considerably.

Efficiencies such as these are the result of ongoing research and development activities, and are showing up in news stories daily. If all industries pursue the goals of efficiency, conservation, and innovation, they will take us a long way toward energy independence. It is very encouraging to see announcements of this type.

Efficiency improvements should go hand in hand with conservation and the search for alternatives. Efficiency alone falls far short of a complete answer to our vanishing energy sources. In fact, none of the strategies discussed here in this book can single-handedly replace our dependence on oil, coal, or gas. New technology that improves efficiency of our machines and conserves energy must be developed wherever possible. The magnitude and the extent to which we have become dependent on the use of fossil fuels require it.

Conservation—The Universal Alternative

Conservation, believe it or not, is our most immediately effective and best alternative to offset increasing worldwide energy demand. Focusing on reducing our energy use is the best strategy for surviving the energy crisis, because it is one in which everyone can participate. It slows the national outward flow of our money that is better used here at home. However, conservation is but a small part of what should become our national energy policy. We will need all of the possible alternatives to make the transition to fuel independence and a fossil-fuel-free society. Because it will be virtually impossible in the near future to become completely fossil fuel free, conservation becomes all the more important to us.

Anyone can conserve, and it will put money back in our pockets faster than any alternative to fossil fuels. The results are often immediate. Conserving energy puts us ahead on our goals of saving money, saving the environment, and reducing our dependency on foreign energy sources.

Large companies have opportunities for large savings. Information technology departments in large corporations operate hundreds, even thousands, of computer network servers, but they are often woefully underutilized. A recent story on National Public Radio (NPR) included an interview with an energy conservation expert, who related how one large company was able to reduce the number of servers in the company from 3,100 to 150. Not only does it save equipment and electric power but also the number of people required to run them. Every business needs this level of scrutiny. It goes straight to the bottom line.

Before deciding what you can do to make your existing home more energy efficient, you should get your home analyzed by a certified professional energy auditor. A professional auditor can do a much more realistic analysis specific to your home. Infrared cameras can be used to take pictures of your home at night that will show where the energy leaks are and indicate a plan for remedying them. Other techniques involve pressurizing the home in order to pinpoint air leaks.

Some power companies can provide this service for you free of charge, but if it costs a few dollars, you will be well repaid for the effort of learning how you can save energy and money. There are also some online energy analysis programs that can help get you started. Your local power company may have this feature on their Web site. Two Web sites that can help you get started are http://www.energystar.gov/index. cfm?c=home_improvement.hm_improvement_audits and http://www. ase.org/uploaded_files/educatorlessonplans/audit.pdf.

You can input information about your house, your family, and all of the energy using appliances and features into a form on the Internet. It requires information you can get from your gas and electric bills about how many kilowatt-hours you used and how many therms of natural gas or other fuel you used each month. When the information is compiled, the program will tell you how your fuel usage compares with similar homes in your zip code area, and how much you might save. It also tells you how much of that energy went to running all of the different appliances, air conditioners, and furnaces. It is not scientific, being based on averages, but it will give you a sense of how your usage stacks up.

Another useful resource is the U.S. Green Building Council (USGBC) that rates new construction and major renovations. The USGBC was established to guide and distinguish high performance commercial and institutional projects. It has developed universally accepted standards. These standards, published under the title of Leadership in Energy and Environmental Design (LEED) Green Building Rating System, give building owners and operators, architects, real estate professionals, facility managers, lenders, and government officials tools to evaluate the performance of buildings. They will be useful to anyone interested in environmental design. The key areas that are evaluated are human and environmental health, sustainable site development, water savings, energy efficiency, materials selection, and indoor environmental quality.

A new study by Costar Group, a real estate information company, has found that sustainable green buildings outperform their peer nongreen counterparts in such key areas as occupancy rate, sale price, and rental rates by wide margins. This is important to you if you need to sell your home.

Search out innovative ideas and keep an open mind. Buildings have been constructed in the same old energy wasteful ways for centuries. Be aware of how products are manufactured. Most products require at least some fossil fuels to produce and transport them to the construction site. Look for those products that are less energy intensive in their manufacture than others. Be aware of where materials come from too. If they have to be transported great distances from where they are made, look for local substitutes.

Recycling Building Materials

There may be local salvaged materials that could be reused as building materials. You may not fancy a house built with walls of old tires, but they have been used in a few cases. Used brick or blocks are a good replacement for new ones if available. The firing and transportation of brick requires large amounts of energy.

As the country becomes more energy conscious, more new products that can help reduce our carbon footprint will be developed for building and renovation projects. Some are more expensive initially, but by saving costly energy, they will prove to be a bargain in the long run.

The Nine Billion Dollar Light Bulb

If 300 million people, representing the population of the United States, each replace just one incandescent light bulb with a compact fluorescent light (CFL), and the bulb lasts seven years* at a savings of $30 per bulb, that is an energy savings of $9 billion over the life of the bulbs, or $1.285 billion per year. That is the equivalent of not importing 25.7 million barrels of oil per year at $50 per barrel. Does that sound like peanuts to you? That savings could be better put to work developing some of the nonpolluting alternatives or rebuilding our energy grid, instead of making some foreign oil producer wealthier. * Life of the CFL and savings may vary depending on usage.

Like the compact fluorescent light bulb, some ideas may cost a few dollars, but can save considerably more than they cost to implement. Multiply all of the low cost and no cost ideas in this book times the number of families and the impact could be enormous. A word of caution: CFLs contain toxic mercury, and if broken should be handled with care. Wear disposable rubber or plastic gloves to clean up the pieces, place them in a plastic bag, and dispose properly at your community hazardous disposal facility. Unbroken CFLs can be recycled at your nearest building supply store.

Light Emitting Diodes

Light emitting diodes (LEDs) are the latest new light source for families interested in saving energy and money. Compact fluorescent lights use much less energy than incandescent lights, but LEDs are the new superstars of lighting, lasting anywhere from fifty thousand to one hundred thousand hours, which translates into five to ten years. They are much more expensive than CFLs, but they are far and away the longest lasting lights with some really great advantages. First, they are much cooler than even fluorescents due to their very low electricity consumption. Only 20 percent of their energy goes to heat, which in turn means less pull on your air-conditioning. Second, they contain no mercury like CFLS do and require no special handling. They can be bought in several configurations including Christmas tree lights. Your family is much safer if you forget and leave the Christmas tree lights on all night.

The variety of LED bulb configurations will undoubtedly grow because they are such energy savers. As demand for them grows, it should soon bring down their high cost. They are available in outside solar-powered landscape lights that turn themselves on at night and off in the morning. LEDs are tiny so that each light or bulb needs several diodes to produce adequate light for most tasks. The more diodes, the brighter the light will be. In spite of their initial cost, they may end up being a far less expensive light than either CFLs or incandescent bulbs because of their longevity, and their lower energy requirements, and their lower heat production that in turn lessens the cooling load.

The latest technology in big screen TVs uses LEDs to light up the screen. If you plan to buy a new TV look at the LED models as they use far less power than either the liquid crystal or plasma models.

An excellent place to review for ideas is the Web site of the U.S. Department of Energy www.energy.gov. It provides a wealth of information, organized in an easy-to-use format, delving into conservation as well as alternative fuels. If you do not have a computer, you can use one at your local library and get help in finding what you need. Your own state's Department of Energy Web site is normally a good source for information about the availability of state tax credits and incentives.

Give Yourself Some Credit

Recent legislation has changed the picture considerably with regard to federal tax credits for energy-conserving improvements. A number of new incentive programs were added on Friday, October 3, 2008, to a bill that extends the federal tax credits and increases the limits previously imposed on them. They make alternative energy much more attractive to homeowners.

As of January 2009 the federal tax credits for all energy saving systems are

- Solar electricity generation: 30 percent of the cost of installation with no cap.
- Solar water heating: 30 percent of the cost with no cap.
- Energy Star exterior doors: 10 percent of cost up to $500.
- Insulation up to local R-value requirements: 10 percent of cost up to $500.
- Energy Star windows and skylights: 10 percent of cost up to $200.
- Ninety-five percent efficient furnaces and boilers: $150.
- Water heaters with 0.80+ Energy Factor: $300.
- Energy Star central air-conditioning and air source heat pumps: $300.
- Energy Star geothermal (ground source) heat pumps: $300.

The good news about these credits and incentives is that they come right off the top of your income taxes, and represent gifts that keep giving for the extent of their useful lives.

New, more efficient, and cheaper materials for the manufacture of solar collectors are being discovered almost daily, which will continue to bring costs down. Other high cost alternatives may require government assistance and subsidies. Tax credits will go a long way toward making alternative fuels more affordable.

A Reality Check

Until the new tax credits were tacked onto the Wall Street financial rescue legislation, things were bleak for start-up solar and wind energy companies. It was even more daunting for the homeowner who wants to help the environment and save a few dollars. Let's face it. Most of us do not have between fifteen and thirty thousand dollars lying around waiting to be spent on something like a photovoltaic solar system that will not return your investment for fifteen to twenty years. Fortunately, the new tax credit of 30 percent for solar photovoltaic will be another matter. The extension of the previous credit, which was capped off at $2,000 and set to expire at the end of 2008, was voted down eight times. It is a pity it took a Wall Street market meltdown to get a partisan Congress to act, but now it is a whole new ball game.

The solution to our energy problems will require very large investments and visionary leaders. The majority of us somewhat resemble substance abusers who need an intervention to break our self-destructive habits. The good news is that the American people, once they understand what we are up against, have always been quick to adapt to what is needed to keep our nation strong.

CHAPTER 20: WAYS TO SAVE ENERGY AND MONEY

The ideas and tips in this section are aimed at helping the family save on energy expenditures. Many homemakers are struggling to provide a comfortable place to live for themselves and their children. There are some ideas for saving energy that even the children can participate in and take to school to encourage other families.

Households of all sizes face the same needs for energy, and all feel the impact when the price of energy changes. Suddenly we all become aware that our use of what we call energy extends beyond just the gas and oil we put in our vehicles or what lights or heats up when we flip a switch. So in effect, we are all in this together, and the good news is that there are things we can do to save energy in nearly every aspect of our daily lives.

This chapter provides you with a list of 135 ways to reduce your energy usage while saving you money. Many cost very little and can easily be done by anyone immediately. Can you change a light bulb? Others may require an investment but in the long run will save far more than they cost.

If you want to investigate other ideas, additional resources are listed at the end of the book. Much of what the author found is already represented here in this chapter. You can also use your computer to check the many Web sites listed under "Useful Web sites." This is such a hot topic that there are new ideas for saving energy posted nearly every day.

Everybody may be surprised at how much can be saved by doing some maintenance or just by doing things a little differently. We all experienced a rude awakening while riding the recent petroleum roller coaster in 2008. The Internet is awash with information about every aspect of our energy crisis, and finding the truth about it is challenging. As with everything on the Internet, look with a critical eye. Those who want to sell you something may not tell the complete truth. Seek multiple opinions and viewpoints.

Your author has culled through dozens of lists and has tried to pick out the most useful ideas and has included some of his own. Many suggestions involve a change in the way we think about using energy. If enough of us conserve in small ways, it will make a very big difference in our planet's environment as well as freeing up family income for other things. Some savings in energy call for an investment. Check them to see which are right for you.

Expense Indicator Classifications

The author is using a $-sign method to suggest a cost/benefit estimate for the following list of energy-saving tips. The good news is that many of the energy-saving supplies are getting even cheaper as more and more people buy them:

$ No cost or a payback period under one year
$$ Moderate cost involved with a payback of zero to five years
$$$ Cost of under $1,000 with a payback of five to ten years
$$$$ Major investment and a payback of ten to twenty years

Savings do not take into account possible tax credits or industry incentives with regard to return on investment.

Example:

SAVING TIP 052: Close off rooms that are not in use, but use caution. Do not close the registers of forced air furnaces. They are designed for specific air volume to each room. Even if a register is closed, the furnace will continue working at the same pace. However, closing the rooms' doors may help keep the central space near the thermostat warmer.

> **DIFFICULTY:** Easy
> **COST:** $0
> **SAVINGS:** Little efforts add up to bigger savings.
> **PAYBACK:** Immediate

Ways that we can save energy have been grouped into the two major categories of tips: Savings for the Road and Savings for the Home, with sub-groupings of related tips. Some tips can make big differences, and some will make only small differences, but all add up to family household savings. The really good news is that if we all save what we can, it will make an unimaginable difference for our country and for our planet.

Savings for the Road

Unless you are lucky enough to live on a bus or rail line, you are dependent on automobile transportation nearly every time you leave home. Only the largest and oldest of our cities have well-developed public transportation. For those people who live in the suburbs, this is a hard fact of life. For various reasons, it is very costly for them to do the normal things we do every day, such as going to work, carpooling, shopping, keeping appointments, attending religious services, or visiting relatives or friends.

Automobile transportation is dependent on oil. The government says that our transportation accounts for 66 percent of oil used here in the United States, and we import most of that from other countries. While drawing boards are full of possible new vehicles that use less oil, or even no oil, many of us are stuck with what we drive and where we live. It will take decades to replace all of our inefficient cars and trucks. So what can we do? For the present, it means getting the most for our transportation dollars. The good news is that there are many ways to conserve on the gasoline we use. Here are some positive savings tips you can take:

Transportation Planning

SAVING TIP 001: Plan ahead for transportation. Make it a major consideration if you are house or apartment hunting. Is it close to work or is there available transportation to get you there without driving? How close are you to basic facilities: groceries, entertainment, or a place to work out? Are there sidewalks?

> **DIFFICULTY:** Map out what you need for the lifestyle you enjoy, and set down a list of key questions to apply to each place you see.
> **COST:** $0–$
> **SAVINGS:** $$$ Major savings are possible, especially if you live in an urban area with public transportation. Occasional car rental may be preferable to owning.
> **PAYBACK:** Always calculate what your driving cost might be from work to where you plan to live to use as a comparison in housing costs. That will reveal your payback. Mass transit may not be a cost-effective way to save energy if you already have a car. It may cost less to drive a car a mile to the store than to pay $1 for a bus to do the same.

SAVING TIP 002: Stuck with your present housing location? Review everything the family needs to do, write it all down, and find the best solution for every type of trip. Be alert for fallback options if the best options become unavailable. If you have to use automobile transportation, make it count.

> **DIFFICULTY:** Convincing everyone in the family that it is important enough to participate. This is essential if your energy savings plan is to be successful.
> **COST:** $0
> **SAVINGS:** $
> **PAYBACK:** Immediate

SAVING TIP 003: Plan your trips carefully. Keep a running list of items you need from specific stores. Group the items by area.

> **DIFFICULTY:** Simple time save
> **COST:** $0
> **SAVINGS:** $–$$
> **PAYBACK:** Immediate

SAVING TIP 004: Where possible, ride public transit, put together car pools, and ask your manager about working from home. Telecommuting is sometimes available for people who perform computer or telephone services.

DIFFICULTY: Check your computer for public transportation in your town or call your reference librarian. Many cities have telephone numbers you can call to find car pools for travel to work. Often the numbers are posted on billboards.

COST: $0

SAVINGS: $ Do the math.

PAYBACK: Immediate

Tips on Maintenance That Pays Back

SAVING TIP 005: Keep your car maintained and engine tuned-up. Fouled spark plugs, low transmission fluid, transmission problems, or dragging brakes all serve to reduce the car's gas mileage. You can do many of these tasks yourself at little to no cost, like checking tire pressure and fluids.

DIFFICULTY: Finding a top-notch and trustworthy mechanic or shop

COST: $

SAVINGS: $

PAYBACK: Immediate and continuous

SAVING TIP 006: Check air filters for clogging and replace them to improve gas mileage by as much as 10 percent.

DIFFICULTY: Moderately easy. Check your manual.

COST: $ Around $15 uninstalled

SAVINGS: $

PAYBACK: Immediate

SAVING TIP 007: Use the recommended grade of motor oil in your vehicle. Using the wrong grade can lower your gasoline mileage.

DIFFICULTY: Check the sticker on the driver's side.

COST: $0

SAVINGS: $ Slight savings in mileage

PAYBACK: Immediate

SAVING TIP 008: Use regular unleaded gasoline; say Click and Clack, the Car Guys on National Public Radio (NPR) Saturday mornings. They insist that built-in sensors adjust the engine timing to the gas in the tank. Edmunds.com acknowledges the fierce debate over the importance of premium but holds to the opinion that the best performance comes from following the recommendations of the owners' manual and good maintenance.

> **DIFFICULTY:** What to decide? Cheaper gas or better performance?
> **COST:** Inconclusive
> **SAVINGS:** $ Perhaps either way
> **PAYBACK:** Inconclusive, but if your engine does not ping, it is probably an immediate savings. If it coughs or pings, then go back to premium.

SAVING TIP 009: Make certain that your gas cap seal does not leak. Without a firm seal, gas evaporates badly. If necessary, get a locking gas cap. Sound unimportant? Think again. If the cap leaks, you lose a gallon every two weeks, and it has gone up in cancer-causing fumes, spewing such toxic chemicals as benzene into the air. Cars older than ten years need new caps regardless.

> **DIFFICULTY:** Look at the seal around the gas cap. Are there cracks or other signs of wear?
> **COST:** $–$$ Starting at about $5
> **SAVINGS:** $ About $50 to $100 per year (52/2 weeks × $X per gallon)
> **PAYBACK:** Under 6 months. A new safety factor. Up-to-date gas caps can prevent leaking gas and explosions from a car crash or even static build up.

Saving through Driving Habits

SAVING TIP 010: Beware the evils of letting your gasoline engine idle. Mileage is zero for idling, and carbon emissions are greatly increased. Do not warm up your car. Your car warms much faster when driving. The estimated engine's idling time cuts mileage by 19 percent. Hybrid or electric cars automatically shut down in stop-and-go traffic because electric engines use no power when the car isn't moving.

DIFFICULTY: What to do in bumper-to-bumper traffic? What about waiting for people in subzero weather? Idling is difficult to avoid, but try to minimize it.
COST: $0
SAVINGS: $$
PAYBACK: Immediate

SAVING TIP 011: Aggressive driving refers to rapid acceleration, hard braking, and speeding to weave in and out of traffic. It is the most expensive way to drive a car. Changing this habit can save you up to 37 percent in gas mileage (average of 31 percent) on the highway. In the city, you will save about 5 percent. You will also be much safer on the road.

DIFFICULTY: Habits are hard to change, but this one is worth working toward. Imagine cutting your cost on the highway by a third!
COST: $0 to change
SAVINGS: $$ A bundle
PAYBACK: Immediate and you will be safer in the process.

SAVING TIP 012: Weight decreases gas mileage. Remove any unneeded tools or odds and ends from your car, but evaluate removals carefully. Do not take out emergency equipment.

DIFFICULTY: Occasionally check the trunk and the backseat.
COST: $0
SAVINGS: $
PAYBACK: Immediate mileage increase

SAVING TIP 013: Roof racks and carriers can decrease mileage by 5 percent or more because of the drag on the car's airfoil. Use only when absolutely needed.

DIFFICULTY: Carriers like bike racks are a pain to remove and put back. It is tempting to leave them there for frequent use.
COST: $0
SAVINGS: $ Better mileage
PAYBACK: Immediate

SAVING TIP 014: Keep your tires properly inflated to save gas. You hear and read that a lot, but www.edmunds.com says they tested it, and while you are safer and the tires last longer, they found negligible difference in mileage gain. Does proper tire pressure matter? Yes. Underinflated tires run hotter and could cause a blowout.

> **DIFFICULTY:** Simple. Use a gauge to match the suggested tire psi sticker. You can find it on the doorjamb by opening the driver's door.
> **COST:** $0 to $0.75, a bargain
> **SAVINGS:** $ Tires last longer
> **PAYBACK:** Proper tire pressure provides better control, more safety, and less tire wear.

SAVING TIP 015: Open windows and sunroofs create drag. While air-conditioning adds work for the engine, tests did not support the opinion that air-conditioning reduces gas mileage (www.edmunds.com).

> **DIFFICULTY:** Be sensible, but comfortable.
> **COST:** $0
> **SAVINGS:** Inconclusive for turning off the air conditioner
> **PAYBACK:** Good tidings and joy among the family

SAVING TIP 016: Allow adequate time to get to your destination while driving under a speed limit of 60 mph. Gas mileage drops rapidly above 60 mph. Edmunds' test showed a savings of up to 14 percent, by holding speed under this figure. Driving 70 mph for a ten-mile trip only gets you there 1.75 minutes sooner than driving 60 mph—hardly worth it!

> **DIFFICULTY:** Habits are hard to change but well worth the effort. Leave sooner and relax.
> **COST:** $0
> **SAVINGS:** $
> **PAYBACK:** Immediate. Your mileage is higher, and your blood pressure is lower.

SAVING TIP 017: Use your overdrive gear if you have it. This reduces the engine speed, which saves gas as well as wear and tear on the engine.

> **DIFFICULTY:** Easy
> **COST:** $0

SAVINGS: $
PAYBACK: Immediate

SAVING TIP 018: Cruise control on the highway will help you maintain constant speed, relieve fatigue, and save you from 7 percent to 14 percent in mileage. Shut it off in the mountains to avoid frequent up and down shifting.

DIFFICULTY: Easy. Read your manual if need be. It is worth the effort.
COST: $0
SAVINGS: $
PAYBACK: Immediate

One further thought: If you are in the market for a new car, evaluate your driving needs. A hybrid minivan may be just what is needed to haul the children around. For those who make frequent short trips, a small hybrid or even an electric, like the Toyota Prius, could be just the ticket. If a larger vehicle is needed for that vacation camping trip, rent one. Think of the day-to-day, year-after-year savings in gas, licensing, and insurance. Play it smart; fit your needs.

Savings for the Home

Start smart if you want to save energy at home. Begin with the energy audit mentioned earlier. You will not regret analyzing your energy use, and an audit of your usage is not as mysterious or daunting as it sounds.

Call your local power company to see what service it provides for auditing your home's power usage. Generally, the company will have a questionnaire you can fill out. They may have a free service where an energy audit expert will inspect your home and tell you where you can improve your home's energy efficiency. In some cases, the power company will even photograph your home at night with infrared film to show where heat is escaping. Your dollars are following that heat.

You can also find help online if you are computer savvy. Try the link http://www.energyguide.com/. Their Home Energy Center will ask for your zip code and help you analyze your home's energy use to find answers to such questions as: Is your home energy efficient? Which appliances use the most energy? How much can you save? Let's look at some things you can do that will benefit you year after year.

In a recent development (February, 2009), the Tucson Electric Power Company (TEP), Tucson, Arizona, instituted a new program called Power Shift. Here's how Power Shift works. First, you sign up for the program, and TEP will install a new smart electric meter. It will be able to track your electric usage, recording the time of day and the power usage for a given period.

There is a designated peak period, shoulder period, and an off peak period. You will be charged for the power that you use in each of these periods at a different rate. In some cases, the off peak rate is half of the peak rate. The periods and rates differ between summer and winter. It will require the consumer to monitor usage or set timers to regulate appliance running times.

A programmable thermostat is essential. Pool filter pumps should be set to run at off peak times, unless you are using it to run a solar pool heater, requiring that it be on during sunny hours. One should, of course, make certain that any electric-powered devices, lights or equipment, are used responsibly, turning off anything drawing power that is not required.

This program can save you money. It is one of the best things to happen in the power generating community, and it will even the utility's demand for power and help coal-powered plants to run at lower capacity. It means the power company doesn't have to build to accommodate peak capacity for the two or three hottest days of the year. That wastes the generating capacity for the rest of the year. It makes us all more cognizant of energy conservation, and it saves us money. It is estimated that the average family uses twice the energy needed for heating and cooling their homes comfortably. How much money could this have saved your family last year? It will save you even more in the future.

Check with the local power provider in your area, and ask if they offer a plan like Power Shift. If they don't offer it, ask them why they don't. Be a squeaky wheel.

Weatherizing

Anything you can do to weatherize your home and conserve its heating or cooling will save you money. Many small efforts will increase your comfort. Some things cost no more than a change in habit, others cost small sums, and yet others are major expenses. All of them will help you save real money.

An investment of $50 in supplies can quickly gain you two or three times the cost of the investment. Caulking, weather stripping, and plastic film can all be used to stop heating and cooling leakages.

Caulking

A caulking seal can be temporary or permanent. Use it when you do not plan to use an opening for some time. It can seal out air or water. There are several types:

Acrylic latex—use inside, easy to clean up with water and is paintable. It comes in various colors.
Silicone rubber—use outside, longer lasting and seals nearly every type of surface. It also comes in various colors.

SAVING TIP 019: Caulk around unused or leaky doors or windows with acrylic latex caulk to seal it off. Tape film to the inside of an unused door or window frame to create an insulating air space.

DIFFICULTY: Moderately easy to apply, but it takes practice to make it smooth and tidy. Have your home center show you how to use the caulking gun. Use the smallest bead of caulk to fill the cracks.
COST: $ Tube of acrylic latex is about $2.
SAVINGS: Two to three times the cost of your purchase
PAYBACK: Immediate

SAVING TIP 020: Caulk the outside of windows that you never open with silicone rubber. A good example is the upper part of a double hung frame. In older homes, a window that is loose in its frame leaks air and sometimes rain.

DIFFICULTY: Moderately difficult. Set the tubes inside overnight at room temperature to soften the contents. Follow instructions on container.
COST: $
SAVINGS: Lowers your heating bill
PAYBACK: Immediate

Weather Stripping

Weather stripping surrounds an operable door or window's frame to reduce air leakage when they are closed. Hardware experts can help you select the right kind for your home.

SAVING TIP 021: Check the weather stripping around your doors and windows. Replace stripping if you feel cold air.

> **DIFFICULTY:** Easy, most weather stripping has adhesive backing.
> **COST:** $
> **SAVINGS:** Many times the cost of the materials
> **PAYBACK:** Immediate

SAVING TIP 022: Check the bottom of the door. It should make contact with the threshold. Usually there is a metal weather strip that is held in place with nails. If you feel cold air at the bottom of the door, replace the weather strip with a new one.

> **DIFFICULTY:** Moderately easy to apply a new strip to a wood door with ordinary tools: pliers and a hammer. Removing the door from its hinges simplifies hammering on the new strip, but outer doors are heavy, and removing the hinge pins requires a small screwdriver or 16-penny nail for hammering out the pins. It is not a one person job to remove and rehang the door.
> **COST:** $
> **SAVINGS:** Many times the cost of materials
> **PAYBACK:** Less than one year

SAVING TIP 023: Add weather stripping to operable windows. Some weather stripping comes with self-adhering backs.

> **DIFFICULTY:** Just peel and press in place.
> **COST:** $
> **SAVINGS:** Many times the cost of materials
> **PAYBACK:** A few weeks of cold weather

Stop Drafts

Stop a draft where you find it. Whether it is air from under the door of a room you have closed off, a weather strip that is not doing its job, or wind is whistling through the loose fit of a double-hung window, you do not have to wait for a sunny day to make a fix for the problem. Cold drafts can be quite chilling even if the room is relatively warm.

SAVING TIP 024: Take a long casing such as a long tube sock and fill it with small beans or rice. Sew or pin up the end and push it up against the cold air flow from a window or door jamb. It may take two to cover the doorjamb. For a short-term solution, stop the cold air with a rolled heavy towel or blanket. A strong draft can leak around your fiber fix, so you may need to weight it down with something.

(Make a shorter rice-filled sock, heat it in the microwave for forty-five seconds, and put it around your neck. It might not stop a draft, but it feels great.)

DIFFICULTY: Easy
COST: $ Little to nothing
SAVINGS: Saves on heat
PAYBACK: Immediate

Insulation

Insulation is anything that acts as a barrier between the inside of your home and the weather outside. An advertisement for insulation used to appear in construction magazines showing a concrete block filled with peanut butter. The text said, "Anything is better than nothing." The R-value in insulation stands for thermal resistance. The higher the R-value, the more effective the insulation. The idea is to fill voids in walls with materials that prevent air from circulating within the wall, setting up convection currents that can transfer the heat from inside to outside. The only caveat is that the material should not conduct heat either in or out.

Radiant barriers contain a reflective side, usually consisting of aluminum foil. They are available on wallboard, insulation batting, and can even be painted on. Increasingly, they are being recommended for additional heat control, not only for attic space and walls, but also for water heaters and other sources of heat.

R-values have not been developed for radiant barriers because there are many variables involved. What is important with radiant barriers is how much of the heat they reflect, either back to where it is needed in the winter or back away from inside in the summer. The Department of Energy has a very readable fact sheet on the Internet. You can read about this in detail at: http://www.ornl.gov/sci/roofs+walls/radiant/index.html.

SAVING TIP 025: Check your roof for leaks. Wet insulation is not effective. Water spots on the wall or ceiling are a dead giveaway. Ice backing up under shingles can cause water damage.

This is caused by an "ice dam." When snow on the roof melts during the day and refreezes at night along the eaves edge of the roof, it creates ice dams that block water drainage the next day when more melting occurs. To avoid ice dams, try to keep roof edges and gutters free of snow and ice. Replace any wet insulation.

Note: Be advised that climbing ladders and crawling around on a roof are both dangerous even in dry weather.

> **DIFFICULTY:** You may want help to check for leaks. Ask someone who comes recommended or whose opinion you trust.
> **COST:** It costs nothing for you to look, but ask for advice at a home center if you know there is a leak.
> **SAVINGS:** $? Leaks have to be stopped, regardless. You may want more than one opinion if the fix sounds extreme or expensive.
> **PAYBACK:** Depends on the amount of damage

SAVING TIP 026: For cold weather, remove window air conditioners and seal the windows with caulk and weather stripping. If you must leave it in place, insulate around it and tape it off. If you feel cold around the unit, it has not been adequately sealed. The unit can also be insulated from the outside with a special insulating cover.
Note: If the air conditioner remains in the window, only the fresh air damper is sealing the inside from the outside, unless an insulating cover is used. The damper alone is not a good cold air barrier.

> **DIFFICULTY:** Ask for advice from your home center help desk if you feel cold air.
> **COST:** $
> **SAVINGS:** Reduces the heating load
> **PAYBACK:** Immediate and outside covers are reusable.

SAVING TIP 027: Fill uninsulated pockets like wall outlets or switches. For safety, shut down the outlet or switch at the fuse box or circuit panel. Wear plastic or rubber gloves. Fiberglass insulation is itchy. Take off the plastic plates, fill the area around the outlet, or switch with small pieces of insulation, using a wooden pencil or chopstick to tamp in the material. Spread it evenly, and replace the plastic plate. Vacuum afterward.

> **DIFFICULTY:** Nearly anyone can do it.
> **COST:** $. One small batt of insulation will do them all.

SAVINGS: Lowers the heating bill.
PAYBACK: Immediate. You have blocked a source of heat loss.

SAVING TIP 028: Insulate exposed ductwork to improve your system's efficiency.

> **DIFFICULTY:** Moderately difficult. Check with your home center.
> **COST:** $$
> **SAVINGS:** $
> **PAYBACK:** Fairly short, a wise payback

SAVING TIP 029: Upgrade your attic insulation to twelve inches or R22.

> **DIFFICULTY:** Handyman level. Do not cover attic vents or recessed light fixtures unless fixtures are rated for contact with insulation. If you do not know, do not cover them. Avoid fire hazards by allowing three inches of clearance around flue pipes or chimneys. Use protective eyewear and body cover.
> **COST:** $$
> **SAVINGS:** Cut heating costs by 20 percent and cooling costs by 10 percent.
> **PAYBACK:** Short term

SAVING TIP 030: Apply insulation to the back of the attic access door.

> **DIFFICULTY:** Moderate. Insulation must be attached to the door, with raw edges of insulation covered. Kits are available for this.
> **COST:** $$
> **SAVINGS:** Lowers heating and cooling load
> **PAYBACK:** Immediate

SAVING TIP 031: Install insulation between the floor joists of an unheated basement.

> **DIFFICULTY:** Moderate. Please note the cautions listed above for attic insulation installation. Most apply. Pipes and ducts may interfere and complicate the process.
> **COST:** $$
> **SAVINGS:** Lower load on your heating, and enjoy a cozier floor.
> **PAYBACK:** Short term

SAVING TIP 032: Insulate any hot water pipes that are accessible, and add an insulating blanket to the hot water heater in an unheated basement.

> **DIFFICULTY:** Moderate. Ask for home center or hardware plumbing advice.
> **COST:** $$ Heater blankets start around $20. Pipe insulation is sold by the running foot.
> **SAVINGS:** Reduced heating load
> **PAYBACK:** Immediate

SAVING TIP 033: Consider a passive solar ventilation air preheater if you live in a cold climate, and your house is tight and snug. Ironically as it seems, air has to come from somewhere for furnaces, clothes dryers, kitchen hoods, exhaust fans, etc.

If you can use the sun to heat that air, you can avoid having to heat that air with the furnace before exhausting it. You can learn about this at http://www.toolbase.org/Technology-Inventory/HVAC/passive-solar-ventilation-air-pre-heater.

> **DIFFICULTY:** There are possible constraints for existing structures as well as possible setback and other building code problems.
> **COST:** Typical cost $10 to $15 per square foot of wall area, including labor and materials.
> **SAVINGS:** Depends on house area and air intake needs.
> **PAYBACK:** Six to seven years for retrofits on existing housing; two to four years if done during new construction.

SAVING TIP 034: Use decorating or furniture placement to offset the cold radiating from uninsulated side walls. Hang a decorative rug or quilt on the wall. Place tall furniture along exterior walls. Place reflective insulation panels between the wall and the furniture for additional benefit at a small cost.

> **DIFFICULTY:** Do not move heavy furniture alone. Invite friends or relatives over to help and pay them with food and drink.
> **COST:** $–$$
> **SAVINGS:** Lower heating and cooling load
> **PAYBACK:** Immediate

SAVING TIP 035: Consider insulating unfinished basements by gluing foam panels to the concrete and adhering wallboard or fiberglass cement board to the foam as a finish material. This is particularly helpful for basements that are partially out of the ground.

DIFFICULTY: Talk to an expert at your home center. Wallboards and cement boards are heavy, and there are tools that will be needed.
COST: $$
SAVINGS: $
PAYBACK: Possibly within a year

Windows

Window treatment is very important for both heating and cooling efficiency and savings. Windows also affect how much outside light can be used to avoid having to pay for electric lighting. In addition to the weatherizing tips listed above, here are some others on making the best use of available light.

According to www.doityourself.com, heat loss and gain through windows costs the United States about $20 billion in energy costs per year. You can find one of the most complete articles on energy efficient windows at http://www.doityourself.com/stry/energyefficientwindo._

SAVING TIP 036: Consider planting deciduous trees on the south or the west to shade windows in the summer but permit sun in the room in the winter. Ask your nursery helper to help determine what type of trees and where best to place them, taking into account the mature tree's shape and size. Do not plant it near water or sewer lines.

DIFFICULTY: Someone has to dig a hole and work the soil.
COST: $–$$
SAVINGS: A well-placed tree can save 25 percent on cooling costs.
PAYBACK: Two to five years before growth is sufficient.

SAVING TIP 037: Plant evergreen trees on the side of your house from whichever side the winter winds blow. A tall hedge can block the cold wind and bounce it over your house.

DIFFICULTY: Someone has to dig the hole(s) and work the soil.
COST: $–$$
SAVINGS: Less heat loss as trees get big enough to deflect the wind.
PAYBACK: Several years

SAVING TIP 038: Block the sun on the outside in the summer before it hits the windows by using pull down shades or awnings.

> **DIFFICULTY:** Handyman level
> **COST:** $$
> **SAVINGS:** Lower cooling load
> **PAYBACK:** A year or two

SAVING TIP 039: Consider blinds or draperies to help you control the heat from the sun that is not controlled from the outside. White draperies or a white liner is best for reflecting the outside heat. Some blinds can filter in light while filtering out much of the sun's rays. Quilted, fitted window shades provide both heat and noise insulation. They are not inexpensive but can be quite handsome by themselves or used with decorative draperies. You can find them on Google under "quilted window shades."

> **DIFFICULTY:** Handyman or drapery installer
> **COST:** $$–$$$$ Varies with material and hardware
> **SAVINGS:** $
> **PAYBACK:** Immediate in comfort

SAVING TIP 040: Storm windows help keep heat out in the summer and retain heat in the winter by creating an insulating air space. If you have them, hang them, and weather strip around them. Consider aluminum storm windows with an operable sash for ventilation.

> **DIFFICULTY:** You need a sturdy ladder and at least one helper for handling heavy glass windows. Acting macho could be life threatening. Keep the children away while you hang them.
> **COST:** $ for a handyman's help–$$$ for new storm windows
> **SAVINGS:** Lower window heating and cooling load by 25 to 50 percent
> **PAYBACK:** Immediate

SAVING TIP 041: Consider buying a roll of clear polyvinyl sheeting to tape off old or single-pane windows from the inside. With small children, take care that the vinyl is heavy enough not to suffocate them if they pull it off the window, and be sure they know how to get out of a taped window in case of fire. The tape need not be unsightly, and the taped window can be covered with an inexpensive sheer drapery.

DIFFICULTY: Consult your home center help desk.
COST: $$
SAVINGS: Lower heating and cooling load
PAYBACK: Immediate

SAVING TIP 042: Apply reflective static cling film to the inside of smooth, cleaned windows to reduce the solar gain or outside heat. Blocks 99 percent of sun's UV rays. Lowe's Energy Solution Center has an excellent set of instructions: http://www.lowes.com/lowes/lkn?SAVING TIP=howTo&p=/Energy/ WndFlm.html.

DIFFICULTY: You will need more than two hands.
COST: $$
SAVINGS: Reduces summer sun by 70 percent and winter heat loss by 55 percent.
PAYBACK: Immediate

Heating

Here is where much of your money goes, and that is true for apartment dwellers and homeowners alike. Homeowners have more control and responsibility for their heating and air-conditioning machinery, but apartment dwellers are affected too. Cooling and heating costs account for about half of your entire annual energy bill. Short of moving in a team of Eskimo dogs for body heat, what can you do to reduce your heating costs and still live in relative comfort? Here are some suggestions gleaned from many different Internet sites and other sources. Remember, not only can you save money with your heating habits, you can make a big difference in the atmosphere. A two-degree difference in your thermostat (Two degrees cooler in the winter and two degrees warmer in the summer) saves the atmosphere from five hundred pounds of carbon dioxide per year.

Saving on carbon emissions is one thing, but lowering your thermostat by even one degree for eight hours will save about 1 percent on your heating bill, and that is money saved. You experience greater savings with each degree you can comfortably cut back. If big sweaters, fleecy sweats, and snug booties can keep you cozy in cold weather, the cooler air will also retain more moisture for your skin and nasal passages. Even the power company wins and can pass those savings on to you. Just remember to pick a wise temperature that will keep your pipes safe from freezing.

Apartment dwellers unite! If you lack control over your temperature setting and you feel you are suffocating, do not just open the windows. Turn off your radiators, and talk to your neighbors about it. If your building is overheated, it not only wastes energy, it is running up everybody's expense. Trust me, you are paying for that waste. Well-maintained furnace and air-conditioning equipment should also function for your comfort. Negotiate with your building supervisor or manager. Why put up with conditions that can make you sick?

SAVING TIP 043: Take care of your furnace. Have it inspected regularly. A maintenance policy can save you money and ensure that it is done regularly.

> **DIFFICULTY:** Make a phone call.
> **COST:** $$ Approximately $100 to $150
> **SAVINGS:** Reduced heating costs up to 5 percent
> **PAYBACK:** $$ within the year and immediate peace of mind

SAVING TIP 044: Clean or replace your furnace filter at least once a month to keep the unit running efficiently. Clogged filters force the furnace to work harder and make it more likely to break down in cold weather.

> **DIFFICULTY:** Simple. Have your service man show you how.
> **COST:** $0–$
> **SAVINGS:** Longer furnace life and less energy use
> **PAYBACK:** Immediate

SAVING TIP 045: Vacuum duct vents and return air registers regularly to keep them clear of dirt, lint, and pet hair and increase furnace efficiency.

> **DIFFICULTY:** Easy
> **COST:** $0
> **SAVINGS:** Decreased heating bill through furnace efficiency
> **PAYBACK:** Immediate

SAVING TIP 046: Purchase inexpensive plastic deflectors to prevent furniture or draperies from blocking supply register airflow.

DIFFICULTY: Easy install
COST: $
SAVINGS: Decreased heating bill through furnace efficiency
PAYBACK: Immediate

SAVING TIP 047: Program your thermostat to sixty-eight degrees Fahrenheit when you are at home and awake and to sixty degrees Fahrenheit when you are sleeping or gone. Otherwise, set the recommended temperatures manually in the morning and at night before retiring.

DIFFICULTY: Follow the manual's instructions.
COST: $
SAVINGS: 10 percent or more on your heating bill
PAYBACK: Immediate

SAVING TIP 048: Consider replacing your manual thermostat with one you can program, and never set it higher than you need. That will not make it heat faster.

DIFFICULTY: Job for an electrician or furnace serviceman
COST: $$ $30 to $60 for thermostat plus labor
SAVINGS: 10 percent or more on your heating bill
PAYBACK: Less than a year

SAVING TIP 049: For vacation, lower your thermostat to fifty-five degrees Fahrenheit to avoid freezing pipes. Some sources recommend forty degrees Fahrenheit, but use your judgment based on your area.

DIFFICULTY: Easy
COST: $0
SAVINGS: Lower heating bill by 15 percent or more
PAYBACK: Immediate

SAVING TIP 050: Consider purchasing an electric-oil radiant space heater for supplemental heat during cold spells. Electric-oil space heaters have thermostats, are safe to touch, draw relatively low energy, can be rolled to where you need them, and lack the hazards of other space heaters.

*Note: Many energy tip lists advise against space heaters, especially electric resistance types. They are reported to use too much energy, cause burns when touched, and even set fires if turned over accidentally. Avoid unvented gas space heaters.

DIFFICULTY: Simple to plug into an outlet, and store the unit in a closet when it is not in use.
COST: Starting around $50
SAVINGS: Lowers furnace usage because it permits you to add heat to your specific immediate area of need instead of turning up the thermostat.
PAYBACK: Less than one year

SAVING TIP 051: Keep the door of an attached garage closed, especially in the winter.

DIFFICULTY: Easy
COST: $0
SAVINGS: Lower heating bill due to a warmer inner wall. Several small savings make for big savings.
PAYBACK: Immediate

SAVING TIP 052: Close off rooms that are not in use, but use caution. Do not close the registers of forced air furnaces. They are designed for specific air volume to each room. Even if a register is closed, the furnace will continue working at the same pace. However, closing the rooms' doors may help keep the central space near the thermostat warmer.

DIFFICULTY: Easy
COST: $0
SAVINGS: Little efforts add up to bigger savings.
PAYBACK: Immediate

SAVING TIP 053: Recycle your clothes dryer heat to add heat and moisture to your environment. Cap off the opening to the outside. Get a bypass filter at your home center or securely tie an old pillowcase over the hose to catch lint missed by the lint collector. In warm weather, reattach the hose to the exhaust duct. Venting to an unheated basement can warm that area and your floors.

*Note: If your dryer uses natural gas, add an inexpensive carbon monoxide alarm near the dryer. Some sources express concern over the possibility of carbon monoxide poisoning.

DIFFICULTY: Moderately easy
COST: $ Uses waste energy
SAVINGS: Free heat from the dryer
PAYBACK: Quick

SAVING TIP 054: Add a reflecting panel behind radiators. Purchase one at a home center or devise one with plywood and aluminum foil.

DIFFICULTY: Moderately easy
COST: $–$$
SAVINGS: Little efforts add up to bigger savings.
PAYBACK: Quick

SAVING TIP 055: Consider buying a humidifier. Moisture makes the air feel warmer and is good for the skin, nose, and throat.

DIFFICULTY: Easy use, but add antimold or antibacterial solution with each fill-up.
COST: $–$$
SAVINGS: Greater comfort and it enables a lower thermostat setting.
PAYBACK: Quick

SAVING TIP 056: Reverse your ceiling fan in winter. This moves air up against the ceiling to circulate the warmer air back down in the room. Fans use little electricity, and the cost will be more than offset by the effect on the thermostat.

DIFFICULTY: Easy. Move the small switch on the fan motor *up* for upward flow and *down* for downward flow.
COST: $0–$
SAVINGS: Furnace runs less.
PAYBACK: Immediate

SAVING TIP 057: Put a warm throw rug under your feet to offset the cold radiation of a tile or hardwood floor. You will feel warmer without turning up the thermostat.

DIFFICULTY: Easy
COST: $0–$
SAVINGS: The furnace will run less.
PAYBACK: Immediate

Thermostats and Heating Zones

Thermostats that take into account the differing cooling and heating zones are common in commercial buildings, but usually not used in homes because of the cost of the additional equipment and controls. An exception to this rule is heat pump heating and cooling systems. Both air-to-air and water-to-air (geothermal ground source) can be zoned. The coolant/heat exchange fluid can be pumped to several fan coil units and controlled to come on at different times.

Typically, the upstairs and downstairs have different comfort zones, as do the north and south sides of a building. Home heating and cooling systems usually combine all zones. Zoning an existing furnace is a major change, and it would likely cost a lot of money if it involved such things as ductwork, but you could contact a heating expert to check out the feasibility. If zoning the existing furnace is infeasible, an estimate of the cost could serve as a basis for comparing your present system to the price and benefit of a new unit.

Fireplaces

Wood-burning fireplaces should be used sparingly if you want to save energy. Many draw more heat out of the house than they produce. Check that the flue damper is closed to avoid heat loss when the fireplace is not in use. An open damper can let 8 percent of the heat from your rooms escape. If you have glass fireplace doors, keep them closed as well.

SAVING TIP 058: Check the seal on the flue damper by closing it off and holding a ribbon or piece of tissue inside the firebox. If the ribbon or paper blows around, repair or replace the damper.

> **DIFFICULTY:** Fireplace handyman
> **COST:** $$
> **SAVINGS:** $$
> **PAYBACK:** Within one year

SAVING TIP 059: When using the fireplace, turn the furnace down to fifty-five degrees Fahrenheit to avoid heating the out-of-doors.

> **DIFFICULTY:** Easy
> **COST:** $0
> **SAVINGS:** $
> **PAYBACK:** Immediate

SAVING TIP 060: Have the chimney inspected and cleaned yearly. Add fireproof caulking inside and out where the chimney meets the wall.

> **DIFFICULTY:** Hire a chimney sweep (fireplace store).
> **COST:** $$
> **SAVINGS:** $ and reduced opportunity for a chimney fire
> **PAYBACK:** Less than a year

SAVING TIP 061: Burn dry hardwood to produce the greatest heat output. Green, sappy wood can cause creosote buildup, which in turn can cause a dangerous chimney fire. Purchase green hardwood a year or so in advance, and keep it sheltered from the elements to have dry wood. Green wood is a savings if you have the storage space.

> **DIFFICULTY:** Easy
> **COST:** $
> **SAVINGS:** Peace of mind
> **PAYBACK:** Immediate

SAVING TIP 062: Consider adding glass doors to seal off an open fireplace. The doors serve to keep the furnace heat from going up the chimney. Without them, cold radiates from the chimney or firebox even though the damper is closed.

If installing a new fireplace, consider one with a duct from the outside to supply air for combustion without drawing your furnace heat out through the chimney.

> **DIFFICULTY:** Visit the fireplace store.
> **COST:** $$
> **SAVINGS:** $$
> **PAYBACK:** Within one year

SAVING TIP 063: If you live for the coziness of a winter's fire, consider installing a sealed gas fireplace unit with fans that circulate the heat into the room from the air space surrounding the firebox. The sealed firebox is a safety feature.

> **DIFFICULTY:** Consult a fireplace expert or merchant. Requires gas outlet in fireplace.
> **COST:** $$$$
> **SAVINGS:** Saving is not the issue, is it?
> **PAYBACK:** Furnace heat savings will help pay for the gas unit, but it will take several years to recoup the investment.

SAVING TIP 064: A wood-burning stove can be installed in or in front of a fireplace. The stove is contained so it does not waste furnace heat, and it radiates much more heat into your room. You can also use wood-waste pellets that burn more efficiently than cordwood.

*Note: Some stoves can be hot enough to burn at the touch and can be a hazard to the very young.

> **DIFFICULTY:** Installation should be done by a professional.
> **COST:** $$$
> **SAVINGS:** $
> **PAYBACK:** Several years

Cooling with Central Air

Air-conditioning can also be a big energy expense and a drain on your income. In hot climates, cooling can cost more than the winter's heating expense, and as with heating, there are ways you can conserve and still live comfortably. Remember that anything you do to weatherize or seal your living space applies just as much to cooling as it did to heating during the cold months. Keep windows and outside doors closed as much as possible while cooling.

SAVING TIP 065: Set your thermostat to eighty degrees Fahrenheit in summer and wear lighter clothing. The difference between seventy-six and eighty degrees Fahrenheit is estimated to save 10 percent on your cooling bill. If there are medical problems in the family, do not risk anyone's health. (See the item on adding fans below.)

> **DIFFICULTY:** Easy
> **COST:** $0
> **SAVINGS:** Reduce cooling load
> **PAYBACK:** Immediate

SAVING TIP 066: Protect your thermostat's accuracy. Keep heat-producing devices well away from your thermostat. Heat from a lamp or TV can mislead the thermostat into thinking that more cooling is needed. Shade it from the sun as well.

> **DIFFICULTY:** If a wall lamp is too near, you may want to rethink the room's lighting without using that lamp.
> **COST:** $0–$

SAVINGS: Reduce cooling load and save wasted energy
PAYBACK: Immediate

SAVING TIP 067: Set the furnace fan control to "on" to help circulate cool air through the house even when the unit is not cooling. Select a "low" fan speed if your thermostat has that setting. Continuous fan circulation also helps dehumidify your home and evens out the temperature comfort zone. Moving air cools better. Using a ceiling fan when you are in a room is an even better option.

> **DIFFICULTY:** Easy
> **COST:** $0–$
> **SAVINGS:** Additional electricity for the fan is negligible and can be offset by a more even distribution of cooling.
> **PAYBACK:** Immediate

SAVING TIP 068: Have your air conditioner serviced regularly. Consider contracting with a heating and cooling contractor for regular inspections. Outside units will benefit from shade. Avoid the south and west sides of the house if you can. Keep the compressor (the outside part of your air conditioner) clean. You can shut it down at the breaker and hose it off with water. Cut away any shrubbery closer than three feet.

> **DIFFICULTY:** Moderately easy
> **COST:** $$ for a service man
> **SAVINGS:** Longer life for the unit and more efficiency
> **PAYBACK:** One year

SAVING TIP 069: Keep return air filters in the furnace and the outside condenser clean. Replace the filter monthly if needed. Check the condenser for any leaves or other debris.

> **DIFFICULTY:** Easy. Have the regular service man show you what to do.
> **COST:** $
> **SAVINGS:** Air conditioner efficiency saves energy usage.
> **PAYBACK:** Immediate

SAVING TIP 0070: Consider an attic fan for your house. It prevents hot air from building up under your roof and helps your ceiling insulation do its work. Even without an air conditioner, it can lower your home's temperature five degrees in a very short period. An attic fan is estimated to cost less than $1 a day to operate. Solar-powered attic fans are a good alternative.

DIFFICULTY: Installation requires an electrician or a qualified heating contractor.
COST: $$$ Generally $100 or less for an attic fan at home centers
SAVINGS: $$ Estimated to save 30 percent on cooling costs
PAYBACK: Depends on the fan and the cost of providing ventilation, keeping the fan from vibrating, etc. The more blades in the fan, the less vibration created.

SAVING TIP 071: Add eave vents and gravity roof vents. This will have almost the same effect as an attic fan without the use of electricity. Place the roof vents near the high point of the roof to create a positive air flow.

DIFFICULTY: Handyman or carpenter level work
COST: $$
SAVINGS: $
PAYBACK: Less than one year

SAVING TIP 072: Do what you can to stop the sun outside the window by adjusting your awning or even moving potted shrubs or trees in front of a window. Any shade helps.

DIFFICULTY: Moving pots may require help.
COST: $0
SAVINGS: Reduce your cooling load.
PAYBACK: Immediate

SAVING TIP 073: Reduce sun or radiant window heat by pulling the blinds and/or closing the draperies. Even if sun does not shine in directly, its heat can be reflected in by sidewalks, water, or even parked cars. The blinds or draperies act as a form of insulation.

DIFFICULTY: Easy
COST: $0
SAVINGS: Reduce your cooling load.
PAYBACK: Immediate

SAVING TIP 074: Turn on your ceiling fan without the light when you are in the room, and aim the air down. Moving the air makes you feel cooler, and it helps distribute your air-conditioning.

> **DIFFICULTY:** Easy
> **COST:** $0
> **SAVINGS:** Fans draw less energy, and you need less air-conditioning.
> **PAYBACK:** Immediate

SAVING TIP 075: Consider adding fans to move air in rooms where the family gathers to require less central air-conditioning.

> **DIFFICULTY:** Easy
> **COST:** $–$$
> **SAVINGS:** Fans draw less energy, and you need less air-conditioning.
> **PAYBACK:** Immediate

SAVING TIP 076: Turn off any unnecessary lights. Get the children to help you limit their usage. Incandescent light bulbs especially produce a lot of heat and draw more electricity to operate, in addition to increasing the cooling load.

> **DIFFICULTY:** Old habits are hard to break, but it will be worth the effort.
> **COST:** $0
> **SAVINGS:** Reduces the cooling load
> **PAYBACK:** Immediate

SAVING TIP 077: Run heat-producing appliances like clothes dryers or ovens at night or in the early morning when it is cooler. Use the microwave when you can.

> **DIFFICULTY:** Takes some planning
> **COST:** $0
> **SAVINGS:** Reduces the cooling load
> **PAYBACK:** Immediate

Cooling with Room or Window Units

Room air conditioners can be added to windows or to walls and are often used in older houses or buildings where ductwork is not available.

For the area(s) to be cooled, the tips listed above for the central units can apply equally well to room units, but there are some other considerations, such as unit location, as well.

SAVING TIP 078: Large room or window air conditioners should be plugged or wired into a 220-volt service line. Ask your supplier for advice. This will draw less current than a 110-volt service line.

>**DIFFICULTY:** Electrician level work for a new 220-volt line
>**COST:** $$
>**SAVINGS:** 5 to 10 percent over the 110-volt line
>**PAYBACK:** One season

SAVING TIP 079: Window air conditioners should be the proper size. Too small is better than too large because the larger unit will run infrequently and be less efficient. It will cause fluctuation in temperature and temperature layering, resulting in less comfort. It will not be as effective at dehumidifying the area. When you install the unit, seal around it with rope caulk to block outside heat.

>**DIFFICULTY:** Calculate the area to be cooled. Ask your home center or salesman to show you units to fit your area requirements.
>**COST:** $$
>**SAVINGS:** $
>**PAYBACK:** Immediate payback in comfort and efficiency

SAVING TIP 080: Location of a room air conditioner is important. It will cool best if it is central to the room to be cooled. If that is not possible, place a fan or two to circulate the cool air evenly. Avoid putting the unit in the sun or find a way to shade it if you can. It will operate more efficiently.

>**DIFFICULTY:** Discuss this with a cooling expert.
>**COST:** $–$$ If you need an awning to shade the unit
>**SAVINGS:** Reduce cooling load
>**PAYBACK:** One season

SAVING TIP 081: Find a unit that has multiple fan settings. Set the fan speed higher to speed cooling. A colder thermostat setting does not speed the cooling process, and it wastes energy. Set the temperature to what you want it to be.

DIFFICULTY: Easy
COST: $
SAVINGS: $
PAYBACK: Immediate

SAVING TIP 082: Put your window unit on a timer to shut off when you are gone and to start cooling just before you return.

DIFFICULTY: Follow the timer instructions.
COST: $
SAVINGS: Reduce your cooling load
PAYBACK: Immediate

SAVING TIP 083: Keep the fresh air vent closed when the room air conditioner is operating to avoid letting hot air in. An open vent will bring in warm outside air and return your electrically cooled air to the outside. Remember, if air comes in, some has to go out. Cool air can be brought in at night by resetting the vent.

DIFFICULTY: Easy. Check your manual.
COST: $0
SAVINGS: Reduce you cooling load
PAYBACK: Immediate

Lighting

Lighting amounts to 20 percent of all the electricity used in the United States, and it represents a big portion of every family's energy bill. Plan your lighting accordingly because it is one of the most effective ways to reduce your bill.

Plan your lighting for each room, taking into account the room's use. The Web site for We-Energies suggests general lighting with supplemental task lighting. See http://www.we-energies.com. People doing close work, such as Mom or Dad paying the bills or Junior studying, need strong lighting to avoid eye fatigue. Planned lighting would include desk or floor lamps to support the close work. This is called task lighting.

For watching television or sitting at the computer, soft general lighting would be sufficient, but when reading or fine handwork is also involved, additional light should be available.

Planning your lighting should also make the best possible use of daylight sources from windows or skylights, and above all, only lights in use should be turned on.

SAVING TIP 084: Turn off the lights not in use. Become a fanatic until it is habitual. Think of it as money for other things (like dinner at a nice restaurant). Enlist the children's help. If there are stairs or other safety issues, use little LED plug-ins that turn on when low light is sensed. These make good night lights. Be energy wise but safe.

> **DIFFICULTY:** Change is always difficult for all of us.
> **COST:** $0
> **SAVINGS:** Lower electric bill
> **PAYBACK:** Immediate

SAVING TIP 085: Install motion detector bulbs in closets or places rarely occupied. The lights come on when you walk in and turn off after you leave. LEDs or even incandescents are better for short-term usage. CFLs were not designed for short period use, and it shortens their life.

> **DIFFICULTY:** Bulb replacement
> **COST:** $
> **SAVINGS:** Lower electric bill, and it is convenient if your arms are full.
> **PAYBACK:** Immediate

SAVING TIP 086: Stick-up lights with LEDs can be put anywhere you need a little extra light. These require no wiring but must be turned on and off with their switches. Properly used, they last a long time.

> **DIFFICULTY:** Easy. They come with adhesive.
> **COST:** $ Low cost and require no electrician or new wiring
> **SAVINGS:** $ These lights do not increase your electrical bill.
> **PAYBACK:** Immediate. Added safety or convenience for little investment

SAVING TIP 087: Switch out incandescent bulbs for compact fluorescent lamps or the new LED bulbs wherever possible. Ninety percent of the energy to light an incandescent bulb is used to heat the bulb's filaments. Never buy long-life incandescent bulbs; they are the least efficient of all bulbs.

CFLs cost more initially. Dimmable ones cost even more. LEDs are the most expensive but last several times longer and give off minimal heat. Some power companies offer incentives to offset that cost. CFLs produce less heat than the equivalent incandescent, which will also lower your cooling needs for additional savings. CFLs come in warm or cool white, as well as yellow light for outdoor use. They are available in many sizes and shapes as well as for three-way lamps and dimmable lights.

Changing to compact fluorescent lamps uses up to 75 percent less energy, and it is probably the biggest possible savings any household can make in the use of electricity. Count the bulbs in your house and multiply it by the expected savings.

Use up your old incandescent bulbs in closets or rooms where the use is infrequent and short termed. Short-term usage greatly shortens the life of CFL bulbs.

> **DIFFICULTY:** Dispose of all fluorescents at your home center's hazardous household waste collection site. Handle broken bulb pieces carefully with plastic gloves, and clean up breaks carefully. Fluorescents contain mercury, a dangerous, toxic pollutant.
>
> **COST:** $ Some estimates indicate that one CFL will outlive four incandescent bulbs that give off the same amount of light. This makes the cost fairly comparable currently.
>
> **SAVINGS:** You can save about $1 per bulb per month on your bill for the life of the CFL bulb, which is roughly three to seven years, assuming average usage.
>
> **PAYBACK:** Begins immediately. Savings may vary depending upon use. Changing out the incandescents is one of the best investments you can ever make and prices for the new bulbs have dropped steadily.

SAVING TIP 088: Use existing dimmer controls and the low switches on three-way bulbs to use less energy. Higher settings use more energy. Use the brighter lighting only when you need it. (Fluorescent and metal halide lights require special dimmers. Changing them can be expensive but will save money in the long run compared to resistance dimmers.)

> **DIFFICULTY:** Consult your home center electrical expert or electrician if you are shopping for dimmer controls.
>
> **COST:** $0

SAVINGS: Lower electric bill
PAYBACK: Immediate

SAVING TIP 089: Use power strips for TV, computers, and other like appliances. (First, shut the appliances down normally.) Make it handy to turn off these energy users until you want to use them. Buy the kind with surge protectors for some additional benefit. Rule of thumb: if a device stays warm, it is drawing energy, and it is a candidate to be switched off.

DIFFICULTY: Changing a habit is difficult; make it as convenient as possible. You will not do it if you have to crawl under or behind things.
COST: $–$$
SAVINGS: Lower electric bill
PAYBACK: Begins immediately

SAVING TIP 090: Buy rechargeable batteries, and invest in a recharging unit. Avoid toys with batteries. Dispose of batteries at your home center or other receptacles where you know the toxic chemicals they contain will be properly handled.

DIFFICULTY: Not applicable
COST: $
SAVINGS: Even stored, unused batteries lose power
PAYBACK: Less money and travel spent for batteries

SAVING TIP 091: Use natural lighting and consider lighter colored walls to reduce your need for electric lighting. Open your shades and curtains in the daylight, if the windows are not subject to sun or hot reflected light. Consider your draperies; do they block out light even when they are opened? Should you change them?

DIFFICULTY: Shades or drapery changes may be expensive and defeat other uses. Heavy draperies may be useful for controlling unwelcome heat or cold. Weigh the options.
COST: $0–$$
SAVINGS: $
PAYBACK: Immediate if no dollar investment

SAVING TIP 092: Consider replacing any of your lighting with light emitting diode (LED) bulbs as they become available. Even track lighting can use LEDs. They cost more initially, but last indefinitely (some sources say fifty times as long as incandescent), and use only 10 percent of the same energy as incandescent. LED bulbs last five times as long and use only a third of the energy of the compact fluorescent lamps. They give off minimal heat. Spent or broken bulbs require no special handling beyond normal care.

DIFFICULTY: Replace them like any light bulb.
COST: $–$$ Many times the cost of CFLs but longer lasting
SAVINGS: Lower electric bill
PAYBACK: Begins immediately and after a short period, big savings

SAVING TIP 093: Make the most of lighting by positioning it central to family use and the areas that need to be lit. Do not waste light on the unused area.

DIFFICULTY: Avoid creating glare or deep shadows that are visually tiring.
COST: $0
SAVINGS: Lower electric bill
PAYBACK: Immediate

SAVING TIP 094: Consider a timer for outdoor lighting so that lights will burn only from dusk to dawn or for whatever period you wish to light.

DIFFICULTY: Easy to operate. Read the instructions.
COST: $
SAVINGS: Lower electric bill due to automatic shutdowns of outside lights
PAYBACK: Immediate

SAVING TIP 095: Replace outside night-lights with motion-detector bulbs or fixtures.

DIFFICULTY: Bulbs replacement is easy. Fixture replacement requires an electrician.
COST: $–$$
SAVINGS: Lower electric bill
PAYBACK: Short period for bulbs or inexpensive fixtures

SAVING TIP 096: Consider solar powered LEDs for your outside lighting, even if it means replacing the existing ones. There is great variety in solar lantern choices. The lights turn on as it grows dark and many continue lighting for eight hours or more. LED fixtures vary in brightness by the number of LEDs.

> **DIFFICULTY:** Simple to set up and operate. They require no wiring and are inexpensive to install.
> **COST:** $–$$
> **SAVINGS:** $ Unlike wired lights, there is no draw on the electric bill.
> **PAYBACK:** The best have relatively slow payback, but the lights are friendly and virtually worry free.

SAVING TIP 097: Send appliances on vacation when you take yours. Turn off everything you can. Set your water heater to the lowest setting and shut off the water supply to the dishwasher and washing machine. Newer refrigerators have vacation settings.

If you turn off your refrigerator, clean out the perishables, remove the ice from the icemaker, and unplug the unit. Prop the door open to permit air circulation.

> **DIFFICULTY:** Keep a list of what you did and leave it on the counter for when you return. In the rush to leave, you might forget what all you did.
> **COST:** $0
> **SAVINGS:** Considerable savings on the electric bill
> **PAYBACK:** Immediate

Water Heaters

Evaluate your hot water heater. About 15 percent of the home energy usage is for hot water, and high efficiency units can use from 10 percent to 50 percent less energy than standard models.

Water heaters are either electric or gas, but those using natural gas are less expensive to operate. If you have an electric water heater, it is all the more reason to use less energy by lowering the water temperature and finding ways to use less hot water.

Consider a new hot water heater if the present one is more than ten years old and you live in a hard water area. Minerals can collect in the pipes and on the insides of the tank. This greatly diminishes the unit's capacity and efficiency. Plumbers report that some old tanks contain such large mineral deposits that the tanks weigh several times their original weight.

New water-heating options include high efficiency water heaters, heat on demand units, heat pumps, and solar water heaters. Heat pumps and solar water heaters function best in warmer geographic areas. Special tax credits may be available for solar hot water heating. Consult your home center or plumbing supply. Some cities have solar stores as well. Here are some other ways you can save on water heating:

SAVING TIP 098: Set your hot water heater to 120 degrees Fahrenheit. This is optimum heat for kitchen and bathroom needs, and it is high enough to retard unhealthy bacteria. Most dishwashers can preheat water to 140 degrees Fahrenheit for effective dishwashing.

> **DIFFICULTY:** Simple. Turn the thermostat dial on the tank to 120 degrees Fahrenheit.
> **COST:** $0
> **SAVINGS:** Lower electric or gas bill
> **PAYBACK:** Immediate

SAVING TIP 099: Run the dishwasher only when there is a full load. Scrape the dishes with a rubber spatula, but avoid rinsing as much as possible. If you have few dishes to wash, consider using a small pan of soapy water and a second pan of hot rinse water instead of the dishwasher. Dishes can air dry in a rack.

> **DIFFICULTY:** Easy
> **COST:** $0
> **SAVINGS:** Electric water heaters represent 25 percent of a home's energy usage. Reductions in water usage directly impact the bill.
> **PAYBACK:** Immediate

SAVING TIP 100: Take five-minute (or less) showers. Showers and bathrooms amount to 75 percent of water used in the home. Remember, not only is energy used to heat the water, the water company uses energy to pump it to you. All water use applies to energy use.

> **DIFFICULTY:** Easy with a bit of planning. Keep the soap, shampoo, and towels handy.

COST: $0
SAVINGS: Lower energy bill
PAYBACK: Immediate

SAVING TIP 101: Fix dripping faucets. One drop per second adds up to 165 gallons per month. If it is the hot water faucet, you are heating water and throwing away money.

> **DIFFICULTY:** Moderate. Check with your home center. Single-lever faucets can get a bit complicated. You may need a plumber or handyman.
> **COST:** $–$$
> **SAVINGS:** Save on your water bill and possibly on your energy bill too.
> **PAYBACK:** Excellent. Begins immediately.

SAVING TIP 102: Consider a water-saving showerhead. The low-flow showerhead should not reduce the water pressure you feel when showering. Low-flow showers of five minutes for four family members saves about $250 a year in water heating costs.

> **DIFFICULTY:** Moderate. With the right tools, most people can change out a showerhead, or you can hunt up a plumber or a handy friend.
> **COST:** $$
> **SAVINGS:** Save on your water and energy bills.
> **PAYBACK:** Excellent and soon

SAVING TIP 103: Save taking a tub bath for special occasions. Filling a bathtub takes up to twenty gallons of hot water. A five-minute shower uses 7.5 gallons of hot water.

> **DIFFICULTY:** Changing habit is difficult. Try to feel noble about the change.
> **COST:** $0
> **SAVINGS:** Lower your energy bill and save time too.
> **PAYBACK:** Excellent

SAVING TIP 104: Wash most laundry in cold or warm water. Full loads save water. Save hot water washes for very dirty or greasy clothing. Pre-treat for spots on garments.

DIFFICULTY: Some garments require special treatment. Use special machine settings for smaller loads.
COST: $0
SAVINGS: Lower energy bill
PAYBACK: Immediate

SAVING TIP 105: Increase heater efficiency by draining sediment from the tank once a year. Turn electric heaters off at the breaker before beginning. Do not force the faucet open. If corroded, it could break. Do not drain all the water from the tank, just the sediment that has settled in the tank's bottom.

DIFFICULTY: Simple if caution is used
COST: $0
SAVINGS: Small energy savings and less stress on the heating element
PAYBACK: Immediate

SAVING TIP 106: Check your toilets for leaks. Put food coloring in your toilet tank and wait fifteen to thirty minutes before flushing. If you see color in the bowl after that short period, you have a leak. A leaky toilet can waste up to ten thousand gallons of water per year. Think of all that energy and your money going down the drain. Consider a new low flush toilet that uses 1.6 gallons per flush. Old toilets use from five to seven gallons.

DIFFICULTY: Testing is simple. If there is a leak, consult your home center or hardware plumbing expert. A new flush mechanism runs around $8 to $10 and is not that difficult to install. The cost of a new toilet and installation is variable, depending on the features selected. Installation is handyman job.
COST: $$$
SAVINGS: Save on your water bill.
PAYBACK: Good on a new low flush toilet, and excellent on stopping the leak.

SAVING TIP 107: Cover a water bed with a comforter to retain the water heat. The bottom of the bed can also be insulated with rigid foam.

DIFFICULTY: Simple
COST: $ Lower electricity bill and longer life for the mattress heater

SAVINGS: $0 Quilts or blankets can be used as well.
PAYBACK: Immediate

SAVING TIP 108: Keep an outdoor hot tub covered with an insulated cover when it is not in use. The cover will help maintain the correct temperature and save water evaporation as well. Turn down the tub thermostat in hot weather.

> **DIFFICULTY:** Covers are heavy and awkward.
> **COST:** $0
> **SAVINGS:** $
> **PAYBACK:** Lower energy bill

Appliances: Usage and Buying Tips

Taking care of major appliances not only saves electrical and natural gas energy expense, but good care and small maintenances prolong the life of your original investment.

Money-Wise Appliance Usage

SAVING TIP 109: Keep your clothes dryer efficient by cleaning the filter after each load. Periodically check the air vent and hose for clogging. Clean air vents and hoses also help prevent fires.

> **DIFFICULTY:** Filters are simple to empty. Checking the air vent and hose may require moving the machine.
> **COST:** $0
> **SAVINGS:** Lower energy bill
> **PAYBACK:** Immediate

SAVING TIP 110: Set the dryer for the shortest time and lowest temperatures to effectively dry the load. High heat is hard on fabrics, and this will also minimize pilling and prolong fabric life. Start by setting your dryer to less than the driest setting. Clothes that come out fluffed but slightly damp will dry quickly in the air.

Climate will affect the time required to dry a load of clothing. It takes some experimentation to find the optimum times and temperatures.

> **DIFFICULTY:** Save even more energy with inside or outside drying lines or racks if this fits within your lifestyle.

COST: $0
SAVINGS: Lower energy bill
PAYBACK: Immediate

SAVING TIP 111: Plan your dryer use to minimize related heating and cooling expense. In summer, use the dryer in the night or morning when it is cooler, and in the winter, run the dryer during the day when it is warmer. The dryer pulls in outside air. You will feel the difference, and so will your thermostat.

Better yet, you can rig a line or use a folding rack in the winter, and let the clothes dry on it while adding some humidity to the air. Fluff them in the dryer if it saves ironing. In the summer, dry them outside if you can.

DIFFICULTY: Sometimes other needs take precedence, e.g., an essential uniform or a tight deadline.
COST: $0
SAVINGS: Lower energy bill
PAYBACK: Immediate

SAVING TIP 112: Dry loads of clothing in succession to take advantage of heat from the previous load. This reduces the time needed to warm up the drum and start drying the next load.

DIFFICULTY: Easy with a little planning
COST: $0
SAVINGS: Lower energy bill
PAYBACK: Immediate

SAVING TIP 113: Set the dishwasher to air dry. The resistance heating used to dry the dishes draws a lot of energy. If the house is air conditioned, this adds more load to your cooling unit.

DIFFICULTY: Turn off the "heat dry" button on the dishwashing unit.
COST: $0
SAVINGS: Save electricity for both the dishwasher and your cooling unit.
PAYBACK: Immediate

SAVING TIP 114: Refrigerators/freezers use a lot of energy, and they are affected by their environment. They should not be placed near sources of heat such as the oven, range, or sunlight.

Refrigerator/freezers should not be kept in unheated spaces. If the temperature drops below sixty degrees Fahrenheit, the unit will draw more energy to operate. The compressor may stop running and even lose the ability to keep food frozen.

DIFFICULTY: Planning is required.
COST: Unknown
SAVINGS: Proper placement will increase efficiency and lower energy costs.
PAYBACK: Unknown

SAVING TIP 115: Refrigerator condenser coils, evaporator pan, and motor must be kept clear of dust and lint to run efficiently. Vacuum the coils and motor or clean with a brush after unplugging the unit. Wash the evaporator pan. Check these areas once or twice each year.

DIFFICULTY: Cleaning is simple, but getting behind a large refrigerator can be troublesome. Two people are better than one for this effort. Most refrigerators have wheels. If not, place slider pads under the feet.
COST: $0
SAVINGS: Lower energy bill and longer life for the refrigerator
PAYBACK: Immediate

SAVING TIP 116: Ideal temperature setting for a refrigerator is thirty-six to forty degrees Fahrenheit and for a freezer is between –5 and +6 degrees Fahrenheit.

DIFFICULTY: Check your settings with a separate thermometer.
COST: $
SAVINGS: $ with secondary savings in foods safely cooled or kept frozen
PAYBACK: Immediate

SAVING TIP 117: Evaluate your refrigeration. A second refrigerator can be costing up to $120 per year in energy costs. If you have more than one, consider turning the second one on only a day or two before it is needed for holidays or guests. As always, take measures to be sure that children cannot crawl inside an empty refrigerator and suffocate. Remove door handles if storing for long periods. In most places, the law requires it.

DIFFICULTY: Not applicable
COST: $0
SAVINGS: Possible savings from secondary units energy use
PAYBACK: Immediate if a unit or two is turned off

SAVING TIP 118: Check that your refrigerator seal is sound. Close the door on a dollar bill or tough piece of paper. If you can pull out the paper, the seal is insufficient to maintain efficient refrigeration. If so, the seal should be replaced, or it may be time to consider a new Energy Star model.

DIFFICULTY: This is an easy thing to check.
COST: $0
SAVINGS: Sealing in the cold air reduces the energy load.
PAYBACK: Soon

SAVING TIP 119: Minimize the time the refrigerator door is open. Opening the doors lets 30 percent of the cold air escape. Take drawers out to clean them. Organize items to be returned.

Avoid unnecessary traffic into the refrigerator or freezer during parties or family gatherings by putting ice and drinks out where they can be accessed handily. If you need extra ice for the party, freeze some trays before hand and store them in bags. Icemakers use more energy because they heat the tray to release the cubes.

DIFFICULTY: Plan ahead and think before opening the door.
COST: $0
SAVINGS: $ Reduce the time the motor runs.
PAYBACK: Lower energy bill

SAVING TIP 120: Make sure the refrigerator is level so the door automatically swings shut rather than stays open. Most refrigerators have feet that screw up or down for leveling purposes.

DIFFICULTY: Leveling the refrigerator feet is not a one person job.
COST: $0
SAVINGS: $
PAYBACK: Immediate

SAVING TIP 121: Load the refrigerator or freezer to allow cold air to circulate freely around foods to keep them at proper temperature. Do not overload.

> **DIFFICULTY:** Simple
> **COST:** $0
> **SAVINGS:** $ and prevents spoilage
> **PAYBACK:** Immediate

SAVING TIP 122: Use the microwave or smaller kitchen appliances. Crock-Pots, slow cookers, toaster ovens, and electric skillets all use less electricity than heating the electric range burner. These appliances are in direct contact with the cooking surface so no heat is lost in the air.

> **DIFFICULTY:** Changing the way we cook
> **COST:** $–$$ to invest in the appliance
> **SAVINGS:** $
> **PAYBACK:** Immediate

SAVING TIP 123: Put a lid on it. Using a lid captures heat and brings a pan to cooking temperature much faster.

> **DIFFICULTY:** Changing the way we cook. If your favorite pans lack lids, consider replacing them or take them to a home store to fit them with lids.
> **COST:** $0–$
> **SAVINGS:** Lower energy bill
> **PAYBACK:** Immediate in most cases

SAVING TIP 124: Fit the pan to the burner. The pan should cover the burner, and if gas, flames should not flare up around the edge of the pan. Too small a burner will heat unevenly and take longer to cook the food.

> **DIFFICULTY:** Building new habits can be frustrating.
> **COST:** $0
> **SAVINGS:** $
> **PAYBACK:** Immediate

SAVING TIP 125: Whether gas or electric, keep the reflective heat pans under the burners clean and shiny to reflect the burner's heat efficiently.

DIFFICULTY: Simple. Remove and clean them, and burnish them with very fine steel wool. Baked on grease can be rubbed off with a baking soda paste.
COST: $0
SAVINGS: $
PAYBACK: Immediate

SAVING TIP 126: Cook with as little water as possible. Energy is wasted while the extra water is brought to a boil. Either steaming or sautéing is a more efficient way to cook many vegetables, and it saves soluble vitamins and minerals.

DIFFICULTY: Changing cooking habits
COST: $0
SAVINGS: $
PAYBACK: Immediate

SAVING TIP 127: Use a toaster oven if you can. Plan ahead if you need the big oven. Start with dishes that take lower temperatures and then turn up the temperature for the next dish.

DIFFICULTY: It all takes planning, and it takes a while for it to become automatic.
COST: $0
SAVINGS: $ Smaller appliances draw less wattage.
PAYBACK: Immediate

SAVING TIP 128: Set your self-cleaning oven to begin while the oven is hot from cooking. Much of the energy in using the oven is in the heat-up period. This will reduce the heat-up time and give the cleaning job an energy boost.

DIFFICULTY: Not difficult, just a different way of thinking
COST: $
SAVINGS: $
PAYBACK: Immediate

SAVING TIP 129: Check your oven seal. Leaking heat slows down the cooking and puts heat into the room for your air-conditioning to offset. Close the door on a dollar bill and tug. If the bill slips out, consider a new seal or a new Energy Star oven.

DIFFICULTY: The test is simple.
COST: $0 to test. $$ Service to change a seal is not cheap.
SAVINGS: $ in energy
PAYBACK: Changing the seal or buying a new oven would vary.

SAVING TIP 130: Do not thaw frozen food in the oven. Instead, seal the frozen package in a baggie and place it in warm water, or pop it in the microwave at reduced power. A microwave uses only 20 percent of the energy of an oven. For chicken and fish, allow time to thaw them in the refrigerator.
*Note: Health specialists object to heating or thawing food in plastic bags or containers, citing that plastic gives off toxic gases.

DIFFICULTY: Simple
COST: $0
SAVINGS: $
PAYBACK: Immediate

SAVING TIP 131: Resist the urge to warm the plates in the oven. Heating the oven to 170 degrees Fahrenheit takes more energy than using an electric warming tray.

DIFFICULTY: Change of habit
COST: $0
SAVINGS: $ Little changes count too.
PAYBACK: Immediate

SAVING TIP 132: Make wise choices when planning to cook. Steak on the gas grill takes far less energy than grilling in the oven, or try pan-searing your meat or fish in an electric skillet. Can you adapt the family favorites to use less energy?

DIFFICULTY: Not difficult
COST: $0
SAVINGS: $ It might make steak affordable.
PAYBACK: Immediate

SAVING TIP 133: Cook for multiple meals. Grill extra chicken, pork, or beef and slice the leftovers for sandwiches or to top salads. Use a lot of ground beef? Cook it up and chill or freeze it in meal-sized baggies. Use it for fast spaghetti sauce, stroganoff, or to top tortillas sprinkled with cheese that you heat in the microwave. Do not microwave the baggies.

DIFFICULTY: Not difficult. If you get caught in traffic, use the time to plan.
COST: $0
SAVINGS: $ It also saves time you can use for other things.
PAYBACK: Immediate

Tips for Buying New Appliances

- When shopping for a new appliance, look for the Energy Star label. New household products must meet strict energy efficiency guidelines set by the Environmental Protection Agency (EPA) and the Department of Energy (DOE) to earn that star. To find out what an Energy Star means for a refrigerator or some other product, go to http://www.energystar.gov/index.cfm?fuseaction=find_a_product.

- Evaluate your present appliances. If your central air is more than ten years old, a carefully selected new unit could reduce your summer electric bill by about one-third. Old water heaters and refrigerators may be costing more than you think. Think Energy Star!

- Watch for off-season rebates or sales promotions on heating and cooling plants. Buy a new air conditioner in winter to get advantageous discounts from installers who are not as busy as in the cooling season.

- Search the Internet for specific answers. An inquiry on refrigerator freezers brought up Energy Star ratings that indicate side-by-side freezer/refrigerators use more energy than top freezers. Top freezers require nearly eighty kilowatt hours less per year to operate than bottom freezers. The bottom freezers were rated the least efficient in energy use. Go to Google and try various word combinations, such as "refrigerator freezer energy" in your search.

- Look for new technology or innovations that save energy, like convection ovens, argon-filled and double- or triple-glazed windows. Be aware that seeing an appliance popularly displayed in slick magazines does not make it an energy saver. Look for that Energy Star logo.

- Natural gas appliances usually are cheaper to operate than electric, and the slight difference in cost can usually be paid back in less than a year.

- Knowledgeable dealers can help you calculate energy savings and a payback period. Write the information down as you go. Be sure you compare a range of prices, features, and brands. Ask about delivery, installation, and service contracts. Ask about tax credits, and check for tax credits online: http://www. energysavers.gov/homeowners.html.

- Read the Energy Guide label and compare the energy efficiency lists carefully among the products you are considering. Write them down with the other product information. Energy requirements can vary within the same company's product line, by model or size. Also compare the warranties.

Miscellaneous

We all need to cultivate a new mind set. Look for ways we can save energy. Not only will it help our country's trade deficit and help save the planet, but it keeps household money in the "kitty" for more fun things. Energy consumption includes more than your home's heating, cooling, lighting, cooking, and cleaning needs. It even includes the paper products and the packaging for nearly everything we purchase, and nearly all plastics are made from fossil fuel. Look for the "Made in the U.S.A." label. All imported goods, which includes nearly everything manufactured, requires great amounts of energy to ship it here. Brainstorm how to save energy with the children. They often have fresh ideas, and it will help get them to buy in on thinking "green" to help the family make the most of the energy that is used.

How much energy could we save as a nation if only half of us really tried to cut back on our energy usage? A lot of money that we now pay out to foreign countries could stay here at home to help us keep our assets in good order. Even small things count.

SAVINGS TIP 134: Buy things that have long-term use, things that can be used over and over rather than things that are disposable. You may pay a little more initially, but not only will you save in the longer run, you save natural resources. You save the energy used to make those items and reduce the amount of landfill if they are thrown away.

DIFFICULTY: Simple, only a little buying discretion
COST: $
SAVINGS: $
PAYBACK: Short term

SAVINGS TIP 135: Save costly energy in your yard work. Use a rake instead of the blower when the leaves fall. An additional benefit is that you save your hearing from the noise of a power blower. Even lawn mowers count. Electric ones are quieter and do not spew carbon emissions into the air. The push mower, of course, uses only your energy.

DIFFICULTY: Manual labor is still manual labor, and it takes more time.
COST: $0
SAVINGS: $
PAYBACK: Immediate

Saving Energy by Recycling

- Reuse and recycle all that you can. It decreases the national demand for energy of all kinds. Even things that are not made from oil are likely to require oil to produce them. Recycled plastic gets shipped back and forth to China as the Chinese reuse recycled plastic to package new items. Much energy is used to ship it back and forth.

- Reuse paper bags as long as possible, and then recycle them for new use. Producing paper bags requires energy and uses up trees that absorb CO_2 emissions, but the trees are renewable. Stores are beginning to give small rewards to people who bring their own bags.

- Try to avoid plastic bags altogether. Producing plastic bags requires energy and oil, a nonrenewable resource.

- Reuse plastic dinnerware as long as possible. Try washing it in the dishwasher without the heated drying setting. If possible, avoid its use.

- Recycle all paper goods:

    Newspapers and magazines

    Catalogs

    Phone books

    Junk mail (Shred anything with personal information.)

    Shredded paper (Put the shreds in paper bags.)

    Cardboard
- Recycle glass.
- Recycle metal cans. Each recycling department or company has specific requirements you must meet. If you do not comply, your efforts will be wasted and the materials will end up in the land fill after all.
- Recycling costs little more than some forethought and time, but its savings come back to you when you go back to the store for replacements. Costs for the manufacturing of our goods are passed on to us, the consumers. Think of it as building a brighter future for ourselves and our children and grandchildren. This should give us all a priceless feeling of helping reduce our carbon footprint.
- Recycling can help your waste management company save money because recycled items can be sold. This reduces its cost which can be passed on to you.

Chapter 21: A Fork in the Road

We have come in this century to that fork in the road where we still have an opportunity to make important decisions. Scientists tell us that one road leads to catastrophic results, and the other leads to a lifestyle that can sustain us for centuries to come. All of us want to pick the road toward a happy, sustainable lifestyle. Unfortunately, we do not all agree on which road will get us there. Politics, self-interest, and opinions get in our way and confuse us about which road we need to travel. How do we interpret the signposts?

One sign points to business as usual, continuing down the same road we've been on since the Industrial Revolution began increasing our dependence on fossil fuels. The other sign points in a new direction, one that is unfamiliar to us. The future is uncertain because we have never gone down that road before. No one really knows what awaits us if we take the new road. However, it is pretty certain that if we take the old familiar road we will experience some unpleasant consequences.

In the debate about renewable resources, you rarely hear the fact that oil, gas, and coal are not our only nonrenewable resources. All of earth's important resources, except for things that are growing, are also finite. We are using up many of our metals and minerals. If we recycle everything that we can, such as iron, aluminum, copper, lead, and uranium, those resources too can be considered renewable, to the extent that they can be salvaged and reused over and over again. If we don't use these resources wisely, including recycling them, someday they will be depleted. The good news is that the vast majority can be recovered unless they are left to deteriorate in the bottom of the ocean or buried in a landfill.

Science fiction occasionally includes mining on the moon, asteroids and other planets, and no doubt there are minerals in space to be had—at a price of course. At the moment this appears to be a pipe dream, very impractical and expensive for some future possibility, but who knows what space travel will be like in a hundred years or so. For the moment, let's get real.

Putting materials that can be recycled in a landfill is wasteful to the extreme. Garbage is an asset that we are wasting. Some day landfills will be mined to recover the millions of tons of waste materials that are dumped there that can be reused, assuming that something has not been built over them that prevents recovery. It is far easier to avoid putting usable materials in the ground in the first place. Even food waste can be recycled into methane or biofuels or composted to fertilize farmland.

The Right Road

We can start our journey down the right road by focusing on the basic things we need for survival. To state the obvious, the absolute bare minimum resources we need are clean air, clean water, food, and a moderate temperature. If we pollute the atmosphere we breathe or the water we drink, we will sicken and die. The same is true if the climate becomes too hot or too cold to grow the food that we need to survive. Moderate temperatures are critical to humans, just like other growing things.

If we all lived in earth's most pleasant climates that required little heat in winter, and no air-conditioning in summer, it would save enormous amounts of energy. It would also be very crowded in those places. A better solution is to find the energy we need to sustain our lifestyle wherever we choose to live.

An Ideal World

Can there be such a thing? Have you ever thought about what your ideal world would be like? I am not talking about a world in which you can eat everything that you like in any quantity, but never get fat. Some of what is laid out here may seem pretty far out. However, can you imagine how our present standard of living would have seemed to people, just one hundred years ago? Our automobiles, our airline industry, our computers and the amazing things that they bring us would have seemed like science fiction, had people known what that term meant.

In our ideal world, we would all have plentiful, inexpensive, renewable energy that generates no CO_2 or noxious pollutants. Everyone would have clean air and clean water.

Homes would be constructed of energy-efficient materials with renewable energy for heating, cooling, and lighting. The environment inside our homes could be controlled by computers, with systems that adjust temperatures and filter the air, keeping it at optimum humidity and temperature. The computers would use sensors to maximize energy efficiency. Dust, pollen, and other allergens would be filtered out of our homes, and genetic engineering could protect us from outside pollutants.

Quality education could be available to anyone, and classes would be offered on the Internet. Highly skilled teachers would be able to teach by way of holograms bringing their knowledge into classrooms and even homes. They will be able to interact with students on an individual basis right in their own homes.

There would still be hurricanes, tornados, floods, and other disasters, but they would be a natural phenomenon, not storms on steroids magnified by polluting human activity. There were massive storms long before the advent of the industrial age, fossil fuels, and burgeoning world populations. Earthquakes will continue to happen because the earth's core is still molten and its crust is still moving around, but better ways to build structures to resist earthquakes will and are being developed. Nature will remain somewhat unpredictable, but our ways of predicting and responding to weather for population safety will improve.

The global economy is here to stay, and an ideal world will still be affected by it. Food production and distribution would undergo seemingly unimaginable transformations, using technological advances to develop new strains of plants that maximize space utilization, water and energy usage and transportation requirements.

Manufacturing would take into account the efficient supply of raw materials and shipping facilities and be located near population centers or raw material sources. Energy for manufacturing would be nonpolluting and renewable. Transportation would be planned logically to make the best use of energy-efficient movement of people and goods. Robotics will play a major roll in all industries. Human populations will be trained and retrained as technology opens up advancements in everything from food production, to genetic control of bacteria, to exploration in outer space. Literature, art, theater, and music would thrive as people fill their leisure time. Technology will provide the opportunity for truly democratic governments and individual empowerment.

In an ideal world, energy technologies would be shared so that all countries would be able to enjoy the benefits of them. Sharing new technologies with all nations might not preclude them from going to war with each other, but it would do much to remove energy resources as a reason for doing so. Undeveloped and developing countries would not be forced to cut down their forests for fuel or resort to fossil fuels. Those trees can absorb rather than create additional CO_2 and have the added benefit of reducing temperatures. Undeveloped nations, as well as wealthy ones, would benefit, and so would our planet.

The generation and manufacture of energy to run our machines, heat and cool our homes, and provide transportation for our citizens would be a huge industry, providing millions of jobs. Energy would be generated as close as possible to where it would be used to minimize transmission and transportation costs. An energy-efficient system would integrate all the possible alternatives to cover the shortfalls of any intermittent alternative sources.

Mass transportation would take people from city to city and region to region on high speed trains, delivering people conveniently to the center of their destination cities. Air travel would still be needed for long distance travel to overseas destinations. High energy density fuels have yet to be developed that are suitable for air transportation. New types of fuel must be developed for this purpose.

Small, car-sized electric units could move people within our cities and be tied to mass transit. Transportation would be cheap and convenient. Automobile traffic would be restricted within the cities. There would still be automobiles for use in areas with limited public transportation, but they would be run on renewable fuels. Most goods would be moved by trains and networked with over-the-road transportation, employing nonpolluting alternative energies. Fossil fuels will be phased out to drive trains as more efficient locomotives using nonpolluting fuels are developed.

If people choose to live in the suburbs, they will commute to work on cheap public transportation, such as light rail powered by electricity. Many people, not wanting to spend time and money commuting, will live closer to their work. Cities would not empty out after five p.m., making them once again the center of social life. Vacant land, and even roof tops, in the cities could be used to grow fruits and vegetables, and fresh food would be available to city dwellers through small neighborhood markets. Buying locally would be preferred during growing seasons. Carbon, heat, and noise absorbing plant life would be used where water permits.

Strides in renewable energy would benefit all facets of life. People will enjoy longer lives from advancements in medicine, technology, and biochemistry. Doctors will have new tools at their command to support healthful populations. Healthcare will be available to all.

Population growth is a wild card that could throw any ideal world out of kilter. In an ideal world, populations would voluntarily limit themselves to what their resources allow. The old methods of reducing population through poverty, disease, and war would be considered unacceptable. How can this problem be solved with voluntary participation? Education has shown to be effective in curbing population growth, but this requires time. How much time do we have? Education appears to be effectively lowering birth rates in many cultures, but there are cultures where education is very limited or even forbidden on the basis of class or gender. Still, in an ideal world we would find a way to avoid a worldwide catastrophe of overpopulation. If population continues to grow unabated there will come a time when the planet's resources can no longer sustain us all.

To get back to that fork in the road, what can convince the people of the world to take the road that leads to a fossil-fuel-free world and away from global warming with its accompanying problems? We must overcome inertia and resistance to change by educating those who are not aware of the bleak future our children could inherit by our resistance to change. Unfortunately, humans do not like change. We like our traditions and our toys. We like doing what we want to do when we want to do it. We like assuming the world in our corner will stay the same. Saving and conserving seem contrary to our nature. Recycling is regarded by many as a chore and a bore. Many of these necessary changes, while saving us money, take some unwanted effort. Is the effort worth it? Not only is it worthwhile, it is absolutely essential to the survival of the human race and much of the planet's animal life.

If we fail to provide any less than the four necessities of life—clean air, clean water, food, and moderate temperatures—the future of humanity will be bleak. How can we secure these things for ourselves and our children into the distant future? At least we must achieve the following:

- Develop cheap renewable fuels that produce zero greenhouse gases.
- Provide some means of storage for renewable energies that produce a continuous supply.
- Provide secure fuel sources so that some countries will not be held hostage by other countries.
- Promote efficiency in our machines that use fuels of any type, renewable or otherwise.
- Encourage a concerted effort to conserve and recycle all of our natural resources.
- Develop a grand scheme to solve the CO_2 buildup in our atmosphere, storing, capturing, or converting it to something either benign or useful.
- Build a new, smart energy grid to provide a clean, continuous supply of energy and serve as a model for other countries, regions or continents.

Finally, we need some means to convince people that we need to keep population at a level that limits growth voluntarily and humanely to stabilize world population at a sustainable level. If we can achieve these goals, we will assure ourselves, our children, and our grandchildren a long, prosperous, happy, and healthy life far into the future. Will it be easy? No, it will not. Is it achievable? We hope and pray that it is.

We, as a nation, have a good track record for achieving many great goals, some seemingly impossible to reach at the outset. We can be the leader of the world in our efforts, showing others how to build a brighter future. A lot of those seemingly fantastic scenarios described above for an ideal world will happen and more. Many are actually materializing as this is being written. Our intelligence and ingenuity will take care of that. Technology doubles every eighteen months. We put men and women into space and landed on the moon forty years ago. Surely the human race can create a sustainable world in which to live. If we have the will, we can, and we must.

Predicting the future is tricky if not impossible, but we can expect certain outcomes if we ignore the warning signs. We know now which of our resources are finite, and we know the rate at which we use them. We can make some predictions based on past behavior. What we can't predict is human behavior when faced with so many variables. While many engage and try to face reality, a large segment of the population seems to be confused and conflicted about the hard choices facing us in the near future. These choices also offer wonderful opportunities for human advancement. We must make a concerted effort to choose the right path, the path to a brighter, more sustainable future.

NOTES AND ADDITIONAL READING

Books

1. *Peak oil* was a term coined by M. King Hubbert in 1956 in his presentation: *"Nuclear Energy and the Fossil Fuels,"* American Petroleum Institute, Drilling and Production Practice, proceedings of the spring meeting, San Antonio, 1956.

2. Hubert, M. K. *Hubert's Peak: The Impending World Oil Shortage.* Princeton: Princeton University Press, 2001. Revised and updated with a new preface by Kenneth S. Deffeyes.

3. Kunstler, James Howard. *The Long Emergency: Surviving the End of Oil.* New York: Grove Press, 2005. This is an unnerving view of where Mr. Kunstler sees us heading.

4. For a contrarian view: Corsi, Jerome R., and Craig R. Smith. *Black Gold Stranglehold: The Myth of Scarcity and the Politics of Oil.* Nashville: Cumberland House Publishing, 2005. This book postulates the belief of the abiotic source of oil.

5. Heinberg, Richard. *The Party's Over: Oil War and the Fate of Industrial Societies*, Second Edition. Gabriola Island, BC: New Society Publishers, 2005. This presents another unhappy scenario.

6. Simmons, Matthew R. *Twilight in the Desert: The Coming Saudi Oil Shock and the World Economy.* Hoboken, NJ: Wiley, 2005. Matthew R. Simmons is a Houston-based investment banker who specializes in oil investments. A somewhat technical look at Saudi Arabia's oil production as it relates to overstatement of the Saudi's oil reserves.

7. Ramsey, Dan, and David Hughs. *The Complete Idiot's Guide to Solar Power For Your Home.* New York: Alpha Books, 2007. In its Appendix B, it has a wealth of places to begin your search for energy information. The book, quite to the contrary, is not for idiots, but is an intelligent guide to solar power.

8. *World Changing: A Users Guide to the 21ˢᵗ Century,* Abrams, New York. This book, edited by Alex Steffen with a foreword by Al Gore, should be on everyone's book shelf. Its 596 pages contain an incredible compendium of information on living green and much, much more.

9. Sharon Astyk. *Depletion and Abundance: Life on the New Home Front or, One Woman's Solutions to Finding Abundance for Your Family while Coming to Terms with Peak Oil, Climate Change and Hard Times.* New Society Publishers, Gabriola Island, BC, 2008.

10. Thomas Friedman, *The World is Flat, Hot, and Crowded,* Farrar, Straus and Giroux, 2008

Useful Web Sites

1. **Energy** or **carbon footprint** is a term used to define one's consumption of energy. To find out what your carbon footprint is go to http://brandeis.edu/energy/footprint.html and click on "Your Energy Footprint." Or go to the Environmental Protection Agency website at http://epa.gov/climatechange/wycd/calculator/ind_calculator.html   to calculate your own carbon footprint.

2. To keep up with daily developments in the field of renewable energy and other new scientific discoveries, subscribe to http://www.kurzweilai.net newsletter.

3. U.S. Department of Energy Web site, a resource for Energy Efficiency and Renewable Energy. http://www.eere.energy.gov/consumer/your_home/.

4. Massachusetts Institute of Technology's *Technology Review.* http://www.technologyreview.com/. Everything you've ever wanted to know about the latest technology. It is a great resource.

5. The Pickens Wind Energy Plan: http://www.pickensplanopportunity.com/

6. The Alliance to Save Energy: http://ase.org, a Web site with articles and ideas to save energy at home and with your car.

7. http://www.consumerreports.org/cro/index.htm for energy-saving appliances and http://www.consumerfed.org/pdfs/saveeng.pdf. The latter site, part of *Consumer Reports'* Web site has a downloadable pdf file with lots of good ideas and more references.

8. http://www.ecogeek.org/ Great place to learn about new renewable energy products and discoveries.

9. http://www.edf.org/home.cfm Web site of the Environmental Defense Fund.

10. http://www.energyquest.ca.gov/saving_energy/index.html This is a Web site for children and has links to other sites for children interested in saving energy.

11. http://www.sierraclub.org/globalwarming/ A good source of information on global warming and other energy related articles.

12 http://www.toolbase.org A comprehensive site for everything to do with the construction industry including building systems, design and construction guides, construction methods, and many other construction-related subjects.

13. http://www.eere.energy.gov/consumer/tips Tips for energy savings from the U.S. Department of Energy.

GLOSSARY

Abiotic: Nonliving chemical and physical factors in the environment.

Abiogenic petroleum origin: A theory that oil is a renewable resource and that it does not come from fossils, but instead is created by a chemical reaction deep within the earth. The hypothesis is an alternative hypothesis to the **biological or fossil origin theory**. It states that natural **petroleum** was formed from deep carbon deposits, perhaps dating to the **formation of the earth**. These deposits are said to be deeper than any fossils could ever have been. See *Black Gold Stranglehold: The Myth of Scarcity and the Politics of Oil*, by Jerome R. Corsi, PhD, and Craig R. Smith.

Alternate energy: All fuels and methods of generating energy other than fossil fuels.

ANWR: The Arctic National Wildlife Reserve. It is an area along the north east coastal plain of Alaska that has been set aside for for potential oil and gas development. It is not entirely a "refuge."

BBL: Billion barrels, usually referring to oil, as in bbl per year.

Biotic: Relating to, produced by, or caused by living organisms.

Biomass: Materials that are living or were living in recent history.

Carbon footprint: The amount of carbon-based fuels per person, organization, or country used per year.

Carbon emissions: CO_2 generated by internal combustion engines or other fuel consuming machines or processes.

Catalyst: A *catalyst* is a substance that initiates or accelerates a chemical reaction without itself being affected.

CFL: Compact Fluorescent Light. A fluorescent light bulb configured to fit into a standard screw base incandescent lamp. They use much less electricity than incandescent bulbs and generate much less heat. They are also longer lasting.

CO_2: Carbon dioxide, a gas containing one molecule of carbon and two molecules of oxygen resulting from the burning of fossil fuels.

Dimmer: A light switch that can dim a fixture's light output with a sliding switch.

EDF: The Environmental Defense Fund. A broad-based international nonprofit advocacy group of business people and scientists.

Electric resistance heating: Refers to the resistance of metal wires or filaments to the passage of electricity. Applying an electric current to the metal element causes it to heat up dissipating the heat into the air, much as your toaster does.

Energy density: The amount of energy per volume of fuel. The higher the energy density of a fuel, the more energy may be stored or transported for the same amount of mass.

Energy Star: Energy Star is a joint program of the Environmental Protection Agency and the U.S. Department of Energy helping us to save money through energy-efficient products and practices. Appliances, furnaces, airconditioners, and even homes are rated for energy efficiency.

Ethanol: Grain alcohol, also called ethyl alcohol; grain alcohol; pure alcohol; hydroxyethane; drinking alcohol; ethyl hydrate. A highly flammable liquid used in beverages and added to gasoline to reduce emissions.

Fossil fuels: Fuel derived from prehistoric organisms: any carbon containing fuel derived from the decomposed remains of prehistoric plants and animals, e.g., coal, petroleum, and natural gas.

Geothermal: Literally heat from the earth.

Geothermal heat pump: The geothermal heat pump uses the earth as a heat sink removing heat from the house in summer storing it in the ground, and then removing heat from the ground storing it in the house air in winter, using a transfer liquid, usually water.

Global Warming: A term used to describe the increase in the mean temperature of the earth's atmosphere.

Global Climate Coalition: A lobbying and public information organization paid by the oil, gas, coal, and auto industry to counter arguments that human activity, namely burning fossil fuels, causes global warming.

Gravity system: Water in a container when heated rises to the top and sets up convection currents causing it to circulate. When it cools, it falls to the bottom and the process is repeated. This process also applies to the behavior of air. This characteristic is what drives our weather.

Grid parity: G.P. refers to a universally accepted cost for generating electrical energy from coal-burning plants. It is usually quoted as $1.00 per watt.

Heat pump: A heat pump is a machine or device that moves heat from one location (the "source") to another location (the "sink" or "heat sink"), using energy. Most heat pump technology moves heat from a low temperature heat source to a higher temperature heat sink. Common examples are food refrigerators and freezers, air conditioners, and reversible-cycle heat pumps for providing thermal comfort in a home.

Heat sink: A *heat sink* is any dense mass of material that absorbs heat and releases it slowly.

Hydrocarbons: In organic chemistry, a hydrocarbon is an organic compound containing hydrogen and carbon.

Hydrogen: The element that makes up 75 percent of all matter in the universe. It is a very explosive element in its pure form, H_2. It is contained in water and many other organic chemical compounds.

IPCC: The Intergovernmental Panel on Climate Change.

kWh: Kilowatt hour. Refers to one thousand watts of electricity generated or consumed over an hour's time. Ratings of generators are usually in kilowatt hours. Your utility bill usually tells you how many kilowatt hours that you used in a given month.

Latitude: Latitude gives the location of a place on earth north or south of the equator. Lines of latitude are horizontal lines shown running east to west on maps. Technically, it is an angular measurement in degrees ranging from zero degrees at the equator to ninety degrees at the poles, written as ninety degrees N for the North Pole and ninety degrees S for the South Pole.

Light-emitting diode (LED): A semiconductor diode that emits light when an electric current is applied to it. The effect is a form of electroluminescence where a narrow spectrum light is emitted. LEDs are widely used as indicator lights on electronic devices and increasingly in higher power applications such as flashlights and area lighting. They use little electric energy.

Methanol: known as methyl alcohol, wood alcohol, wood naphtha or wood spirits. It is the simplest alcohol, and is a toxic liquid similar to ethanol (drinking alcohol). It can be used as biodiesel.

NIPCC: The Nongovernmental International Panel on Climate Change, a group that refutes the effect of human activity on climate change.

Northwest Passage: An ocean route from the Atlantic to the Pacific passing north of Canada through the Arctic along a path that is usually frozen year around.

NREL: National Renewable Energy Laboratory, located at Sandia Laboratory in Albuquerque, New Mexico. Their mission is to develop renewable energy and energy efficiency technologies and practices, advance related science and engineering, and transfer knowledge and innovations to address the nation's energy and environmental goals.

Offshore: Oil drilling term referring to drilling platforms located offshore, sometimes many miles at sea.

OPEC: The Organization of Petroleum Exporting Countries, consisting of seven Arab countries plus Iran, Ecuador, Indonesia, Angola, Venezuela, and Nigeria.

Parabolic collectors: Parabola-shaped curved mirrors that focus the sun's rays at a point in space generating great heat. A parabola is the geometric term for the shape that a chain or rope takes when suspended from both ends.

Payback period: Period in which the initial cost of an improvement can be returned through savings realized by the improvement, often called return on investment (ROI).

Peak oil: The point in time at which half of the earth's recoverable oil reserves are pumped from all known existing wells. It is the point at which production will begin to decline, regardless of secondary or tertiary recovery methods employed. It is roughly expressed graphically as the highest point on a bell-shaped curve, representing peak production in number of barrels and identified by a date.

Photovoltaic (PV): A photovoltaic system is a system that uses solar cells to convert sunlight into electricity.

Power strip: A strip of multiple electric outlets, often with a surge protector, into which multiple electrical devices or computer accessories can be plugged and turned on or off with one switch. They plug into a single wall outlet.

Renewable resources: Resources that are self-renewable, like forests, corn, switch grass, or wood manufacturing waste. See biomass.

Solar farm: A large group of photovoltaic or focusing parabolic solar collectors.

Turbine: Refers to a machine or motor that generates electricity. They operate much like the generator in your car to generate electricity, except a fluid medium, such as air or water, passes over propeller blades causing the engine to rotate.

Unconventional oil sources: Refers to oil coming from sources other than drilled wells, such as oil bearing sands and shale.

Wind farm: Usually a large group of wind-powered generators or windmills.

About The Author

Phillip J. Greene, M. Arch, MBA

Phillip Greene is a retired architect with 45 years of experience. His design projects varied widely from university buildings to animal habitats for theme parks to individual homes. He was also responsible for site and master planning as well as building design. His client list was diverse, including Busch Entertainment Corporation, Universal Studios, the Army Corps of Engineers and the University of Illinois.

While the energy crisis of 1973 awakened him to the urgency of gas and oil resource conservation, it was not a new interest. The author has vivid memories of World War II in the 1940s during which Americans recycled everything from rendered kitchen fat and oil to scrap metals. Because of wartime scarcity, rationing included gasoline, tires, shoes, canned food, meat and butter. Greene well remembers the huge piles of scrap metals on a vacant lot near his home, as well as the family Victory Garden for which he was designated family gardener. He is fully aware of what is required when populations face scarcity.

Greene was moved to write this book when a search for information about current and future energy requirements revealed so many conflicting voices. There are many books about particular energy resources or topics, some that appeared insightful and others that appeared to press some particular political partisanship or industry interest. There seemed to be no single book that incorporated the energy possibilities available to an average person who sincerely wants to understand what is real and what is not in terms that anyone can understand. Everything seemed a tangle of opinion about resource availability and the state of the planet's environment. Was there global warming, were humans to blame, and was there really even an oil crisis?

With that in mind, he sat down to write that book with what he could glean from the libraries and the internet, mixed in with common sense. In the end, he came to feel there are many real dangers but also wonderful opportunities for the human race and this planet.

INDEX

Coal fired power-generating generating plants, 53, 54
Cold fusion, 93, 94
Colorado River Basin, 74
Columbia, (River dam), 74
Compact fluorescent lamps, (CFL), 146
Compressed Natural gas, 96, 97
Corn, 79
Costar Group, 109
Cost, Avoided, 38
    Wholesale, 38
Cogeneration, 99
Combined heat and power, 99
Commercial bulk hydrogen, 83
Compact fluorescent light, (CFL), 110, 111
Computer network servers, 108
Congressional Budget Office, 10
Conservation, 107, 108
Crude oil, 4

D
Dana Christensen, 93
Decommissioning (nuclear power plants), 89
Deforestation, 80
Department of Energy, 36
Depleted wells, 9
Dimmer controls, 147
Dirty bombs, 90
Dishwasher, 151, 155
Dryer, clothes, 136

E
Earth sheltered, 50
Earth protected, 50
Eave vents, 142
Economy, the, 4
Education, 169
Efficiency incentives, 39
Efficiency improvements, 108
Efficiency, 170

R

6376152R0

Made in the USA
Charleston, SC
17 October 2010